Heaven, Hell, . . . and Purgatory?

The Pro Ecclesia Series

Books in The Pro Ecclesia Series are "for the Church." The series is sponsored by the Center for Catholic and Evangelical Theology, founded by
Carl Braaten and Robert Jenson in 1991. The series seeks to nourish the
Church's faithfulness to the gospel of Jesus Christ through a theology that
is self-critically committed to the biblical, dogmatic, liturgical, and ethical traditions that form the foundation for a fruitful ecumenical theology.
The series reflects a commitment to the classical tradition of the Church as
providing the resources critically needed by the various churches as they
face modern and post-modern challenges. The series will include books by
individuals as well as collections of essays by individuals and groups. The
Editorial Board will be drawn from various Christian traditions.

OTHER TITLES IN THE SERIES INCLUDE:

- *The Morally Divided Body: Ethical Disagreement and the Disunity of
  the Church*, edited by Michael Root and James J. Buckley

- *Christian Theology and Islam*, edited by Michael Root and James J.
  Buckley

- *Who Do You Say That I Am?: Proclaiming and Following Jesus Today*,
  edited by Michael Root and James J. Buckley

- *What Does It Mean to "Do This"? Supper, Mass, Eucharist*, edited by
  Michael Root and James J. Buckley

Heaven, Hell, . . . and Purgatory?

Edited by

Michael Root &
James J. Buckley

CASCADE *Books* · Eugene, Oregon

HEAVEN, HELL, . . . AND PURGATORY?

Pro Ecclesia Series 5

Cascade Books
An Imprint of Wipf and Stock Publishers
199 W. 8th Ave., Suite 3
Eugene, OR 97401

www.wipfandstock.com

ISBN 13: 978-1-4982-0105-6

Cataloguing-in-Publication Data

Heaven, hell, . . . and purgatory? / edited by Michael Root and James J. Buckley.

x + 92 p. ; 23 cm. Includes bibliographical references.

Pro Ecclesia Series 5

ISBN 13: 978-1-4982-0105-6

1. Future life—History of doctrines. 2. Heaven. 3. Hell. 4. Purgatory. I. Title. II. Series.

BL535 H35 2015

Manufactured in the U.S.A.   09/14/2015

Contents

Contributors

Victor Lee Austin, a priest in the Episcopal Church, is theologian-in-residence at Saint Thomas Church Fifth Avenue in New York City. He was previously rector of a parish for fourteen years, and has also taught at Mount Aloysius College, Fordham University, the General Theological Seminary, and elsewhere. His book *Up with Authority: Why We Need Authority to Flourish as Human Beings* (2010) was shortlisted for the Michael Ramsey Prize in Theological Writing. His latest book is *Christian Ethics: A Guide for the Perplexed* (2012).

James J. Buckley is Professor of Theology at Loyola University Maryland. He is a member of the North American Lutheran Catholic dialogue and an associate director of the Center for Catholic and Evangelical Theology. He contributed to and edited *The Blackwell Companion to Catholicism* (2008).

Paul J. Griffiths is Warren Professor of Catholic Theology at Duke University's Divinity School. He is the author of many essays and books, most recently *Decreation: The Last Things of All Creatures* (2014), and *The Song of Songs: A Commentary* (2011).

Isabel Moreira is Professor of History at the University of Utah. She has published widely on religion, hagiography, and society in late antiquity and the early Middle Ages. Her publications include *Heaven's Purge: Purgatory in Late Antiquity* (2010), and *Dreams, Visions and Spiritual Authority in Merovingian Gaul* (2000). She is also the coeditor of *Hell and Its Afterlife: Historical and Contemporary Perspectives* (2010). She currently serves as Chair of the History Department at the University of Utah.

Michael Root is Professor of Systematic Theology at The Catholic University of America and Executive Director of the Center for Catholic and Evangelical Theology. He was formerly the Director of the Institute for Ecumenical Research, Strasbourg, France.

Jerry L. Walls is Scholar in Residence in the philosophy department at Houston Baptist University. He has authored or edited more than a dozen books and more than eighty articles and reviews. Among his books are *Hell: The Logic of Damnation* (1992); *Heaven: The Logic of Eternal Joy* (2002); *Purgatory: The Logic of Total Transformation* (2012); and, as editor, *The Oxford Handbook of Eschatology* (2008).

Ralph Wood serves as University Professor of Theology and Literature at Baylor University. His main appointment is in Religion, but he also teaches in Great Texts and English. His main books are *The Comedy of Redemption* (1988), *Contending for the Faith* (2003), *The Gospel According to Tolkien* (2004), *Flannery O'Connor and the Christ-Haunted South* (2004), and *Chesterton: The Nightmare Goodness of God* (2011).

David S. Yeago is Adjunct Professor of Lutheran Studies at the Charlotte, NC, campus of Gordon-Conwell Theological Seminary.

Preface

Michael Root and James J. Buckley

WHAT IS OUR DESTINY? The final end of humanity and the universe is a subject of perennial interest, especially for Christians. What are we promised? Will anyone finally be left out of God's intentions to bless humanity? What sort of transformation will be needed to enter the presence of God? These questions have been at the heart of Christian teachings about last things. The 2013 Pro Ecclesia conference of the Center for Catholic and Evangelical Theology focused such issues on the theme "Heaven, Hell, . . . and Purgatory?"

The theme is obviously central to any Catholic and Evangelical theology both because of its intrinsic importance to the scriptural tradition and because they were and are matters of dispute among Christians—in the sixteenth century and today. One lesson of decades of dialogue is that we cannot dispute what can only be disputed. We need to carry out our disputes on the basis of what we take to be our common ground, our communion in the faith. We thus do not here take up the traditional disputes seriatim, although there is plenty of thought here for dealing with those disputes. For a sample of a successful common statement on such disputed issues, readers can consult the eleventh round of the U.S. Lutheran-Catholic dialogue.[1] Our authors here are our usual mix of different sorts of folks interested in contributing to a Catholic and Evangelical theology, from academies and seminaries and congregations, all interested in the pastoral and practical

1. Lowell G. Almen and Richard J. Sklba, eds., *The Hope of Eternal Life. Lutherans and Catholics in Dialogue XI. Common Statement of the Eleventh Round of the U.S, Lutheran-Catholic Dialogue* (Minneapolis: Lutheran University Press, 2011).

context of all good thinking, including theology. David Yeago and Victor Lee Austin bookend the collection—the first providing the evangelical horizon for our last judgment and the latter samples of how to preach heaven and hell. Inside those bookends, Paul Griffiths and Jerry Walls provide the different perspectives of two practicing philosophers on what is going on in heaven, and hell. The two central chapters are by a historian (Isabel Moreira) revising our ideas of where purgatory came from and a literary critic (Ralph Wood) laying out Walker Percy's funny and frightening vision of hell and purgatory as already present in our culture. The end result, we hope, is a sample of how heaven and hell (and purgatory) shape the lives of preachers and congregations, of philosophical as well as dogmatic theologians, and of fiction writers who also write, of course, about the real world of the triune God of Jesus Christ.

Michael Root, Catholic University of America

James J. Buckley, Loyola University Maryland

1

The Christian Faith and the Horizon of Judgment

David S. Yeago

IN HIS DIALOGUE ON *The Ascetic Life*, St. Maximus the Confessor presents an exchange between an old monk and a young brother seeking instruction. The old man sets forth many classic themes of eastern monastic spirituality in light of the opening question of the dialogue: "Please, Father, tell me: What was the purpose of the Lord's becoming man?" But somewhere around the halfway mark the tone and character of the work change. In answer to the young brother's question, "Father, why do I have no compunction?" the old man bursts forth in a lengthy jeremiad that fills much of the rest of the work:

> And the old man answered: "Because there is no fear of God before our eyes, because we have become a resting-place of all evils, and, for that reason, we scorn as a mere thought the dreadful punishment of God. For who does not feel compunction at hearing Moses speaking about sinners in God's person: *A fire is kindled in my wrath, it shall burn to the lowest hell. It shall devour the earth and her increase; it shall burn the foundations of the mountains. I will heap evils upon them, and will spend my arrows upon them* (Deut 32:22f.)?"[1]

1. St. Maximus the Confessor, *The Ascetic Life; The Four Centuries on Charity,*

Similar and lengthy citations follow from Isaiah, Jeremiah, Ezekiel, Daniel, the Psalms; this first catena ends with the words of St. Paul, "For we must all stand before the judgment seat of Christ, so that every one of us may receive reward for things done through the body, whether good or evil."[2] The old man's speech continues over many pages, turning from denunciation to prayer, at every point drawing extensively from the Scriptures, until the young brother, "having heard all this and being deeply struck with compunction," asks in tears: "From what I see, Father, there is no hope of salvation left me. 'For my iniquities have gone over my head' (Ps 37:5). Yet I entreat you, tell me what I ought to do?"

> Then the old man answered and said, "With men salvation is impossible; but with God all things are possible" [Matt 1:52], as the Lord Himself has said. Therefore "let us come before His presence in contrition and thanksgiving; let us adore and fall down and weep before the Lord that made us, for He is our God." (Ps 94:2, 6; LXX)[3]

Now, I must sadly confess that when I read this dialogue years ago, my first reaction was not to weep for my sins but rather to think, "Take that, Krister Stendahl! You can't blame that on Augustine—it must be the introspective conscience of the *East*."[4] While this might lead us to sobering reflection on whether professors in particular can be saved, I want to respond a bit more appropriately this time around, and take the old man's words as a starting point for reflection on the Christian faith and the horizon of judgment.

By the "horizon of judgment" I mean just what the old man's speech brings so vividly before us. The Christian faith as it is attested in the Scriptures and in ecumenical tradition includes the expectation that Christ "will come again to judge the living and the dead." Traditional Christianity is lived out in the awareness that all human creatures stand under the pressure of God's unyielding demand for righteousness, that we are utterly

---

translated and edited by Polycarp Sherwood, Ancient Christian Writers 21 (Westminster, MD: Newman, 1955) 118.

2. Ibid., 118–20.

3. Ibid., 130.

4. Cf. Krister Stendahl, "Paul and the Introspective Conscience of the West," in *Paul Among Jews and Gentiles* (Philadelphia: Fortress, 1976) 78–96. Stendahl argued that the whole tradition of western Pauline interpretation was based on a misunderstanding, rooted in Augustine's illegitimate use of Paul's thought to address his own inner anxieties.

exposed to his scrutiny, and that we go to meet a final judgment in which all wickedness and evil will be terminated once and for all. This is the "horizon of judgment."

It is no secret that in the last century this horizon largely faded from the awareness of the mainline Christianity of the Global North. H. Richard Niebuhr's gibe is worth repeating for perhaps the millionth time: "A God without wrath brought men without sin into a Kingdom without judgment through the ministrations of a Christ without a Cross."[5] In one of the most profound Lutheran essays on justification written in the last century, the Heidelberg theologian Peter Brunner wrote of the way in which the Reformation doctrine presupposed an eschatology of judgment that has become alien to modern Christianity:

> We must be clear that the sharp point is broken off the message of justification from the start and its power is taken away, if it does not direct the gaze of its hearer clearly and unambiguously to the last things, to our passage through the verdict of Jesus Christ in the Last Judgment. Justification by faith has to do, decisively and in the first instance, with what will meet us from God's side after this life, when we have died, with what will meet us after this whole earthly history, when this earth and this heaven will be no more.[6]

This message has largely become unintelligible, Brunner writes, in a culture marked not so much by dogmatic atheism as by a "dominant *Lebensgefühl*," a "feel" for life and a "style of living" that no longer takes account of God. This culture "has, viewed as a whole, imprisoned itself in the immanence of its understanding of existence as in a prison. It no longer has any vision that reaches beyond itself. It feels itself alone in the world without God as counterpart."[7] In this situation, the life and ministry of the churches has changed dramatically.

> What do the people who still belong to the church expect from the Christian faith? What are they looking for in the church? Is it not very commonly spiritual help for daily life? We want to be better equipped to cope with the difficulties of our personal life. We

---

5. H. Richard Niebuhr, *The Kingdom of God in America* (New York: Harper and Row, 1959) 193.

6. Peter Brunner, "'Rechtfertigung' heute: Versuch einter dogmatischen Paraklese," in Brunner, *Pro Ecclesia: Gesammelte Aufsätze zur dogmatischen Theologie*, 2nd ed., Band 2 (Flacius-Verlag, 1990) 127. This essay was written in 1962.

7. Ibid., 125.

want to overcome these and those bad inclinations in ourselves. We would like to become better people. We would like to have something stable on which we can rely when we are threatened by trouble, sickness, misfortune, and temptations. We would like to experience something of joy and real community in this lonely and sorrowful world.[8]

In the same way, the diaconal engagement with human need has become the "normative function" of the existence of many churches, while the promise of eternal life in Christ has become at best an awkward heritage:

It seems likely that many church leaders, many church administrations, many church synods, many church delegations, but also many congregations of the church, would be very much surprised if one told them that the church, even this very Evangelical Lutheran territorial church of theirs, is an *institute for salvation* (*Heilsanstalt*) and that the real meaning and goal of this church consists in throwing the life-belt which God has entrusted to it into the ocean of lostness, so that human beings may be snatched from eternal death and eternal damnation by this life-belt and rescued for eternal life and eternal beatitude![9]

Brunner by no means despised either spiritual help in daily life or the church's diaconal help to those in need; his point is that these necessary ministries look and function differently when they are pursued within the horizon of eschatological judgment. I have been told recently of at least one mainline denomination whose disaster relief workers are prohibited from speaking about Jesus or engaging in prayer with those whom they are attempting to help—a fairly advanced development of the condition Brunner described.

In the body of this paper, I would like simply to reflect on the horizon of judgment within which historic Christianity operates. I hope to do so without entering into debates about universal salvation or the nature of damnation or the doctrine of purgatory, though what I say may be relevant to those discussions. I will freely confess that I am not certain whether this presentation is an academic lecture or a sermon or something in between. I shall in any case proceed by considering four theses.

8. Ibid., 126.

9. Ibid., 127

I. God's final judgment means that all things are put to rights, truth is established, and evil is terminated.

In the Old Testament, the theme of judgment is tied closely to one particular strand of usage of the word *mishpat*, which is often translated "judgment." The strand of usage I have in mind speaks of *mishpat* as an action, as in the expression "do *mishpat*." Generally speaking, the doing or executing of *mishpat* is the action of a ruler putting a bad situation to rights; in this broad sense it has a wide range of applications and is translated in a wide variety of ways. In its forensic usage, the execution of *mishpat* is not so much like pronouncing the verdict of guilty or non-guilty in a modern criminal court; it is more like the judgment in a civil suit in which a disorder or inequity is both identified and corrected. In the paradigmatic narrative of the *mishpat* of Solomon in 1 Kings 5, there is no mention of any punishment meted out to the woman who sought to steal the other woman's child—but the truth is established and the situation is put to rights, so that the true mother is reunited with her child.

God's judgment is likewise God's action putting to rights a situation that has become intolerable. "I know that the Lord will maintain the cause of the afflicted, and will execute justice for the needy" (Ps 140:12).[10] When the wealthy oppress the poor, when the nations oppress Israel, when Israel dishonors God, the divine judgment discloses the truth of the situation and sets things right.

Much of recent biblical theology has wanted to identify the righteousness which God establishes by judgment with simple covenant faithfulness, so that God's commitment to judgment comes down to his loyalty to his people or indeed to his creatures as a whole. But covenant faithfulness is not that simple in the Old Testament. Rescuing Israel not only involves the destruction of Israel's enemies, but also the doom of many Israelites, as in Isa 4:

> In that day the branch of the Lord shall be beautiful and glorious, and the fruit of the land shall be the pride and the honor of the survivors of Israel. And he who is left in Zion and remains in Jerusalem shall be called holy, everyone who has been recorded for life in Jerusalem, when the Lord shall have washed away the filth of the daughters of Zion and cleansed the bloodstains of Jerusalem from its midst by a spirit of *mishpat* and a spirit of burning. (Isa 4:2–4)

10. Biblical passages are cited according to the English Standard Version.

The oracles of judgment in Isaiah 3 on the powerful men and women of Jerusalem are not mitigated at all by this oracle of salvation; it is the *survivors* of Israel who will be blessed, those who are still standing after Jerusalem has been scoured and purified with the spirit of judgment and the spirit of burning.

Adolf Schlatter, still the most trenchant theological critic of standard Protestant readings of Paul, nonetheless described the simple equation of God's righteousness with covenant-faithfulness as "taking the 'right' out of 'righteousness.'" That is, it removes the term from its judgment-setting, and suppresses the note of "contradiction against wickedness" inherent in that context.[11] The judgment of God is not the judgment of the Dodo-Bird in *Alice*: "At last the Dodo said, '*everybody* has won, and all must have prizes.'" The divine judgment is inexorable in exposing truth and in terminating evil. The prophecy of a *Last* Judgment, a *final* putting-to-rights of creation, means that in the end *every* lie will be exposed and *no* evil will be tolerated.

The great consolations of the concluding chapters of St. John's Apocalypse likewise not only include but in a real sense depend upon other passages that are less welcoming. It is intrinsic to the promise of the New Jerusalem, to the wiping away of every tear and the shining of God's glory, that "nothing unclean will ever enter it, nor anyone who does what is detestable or false" (Rev 21:27) that dogs and sorcerers and fornicators and murderers and idolaters, "and everyone who loves and practices falsehood" (Rev 22:15) will be left outside. Include not only the murderers, but even those who love and practice falsehood, and the tears will flow again before the nations finish their triumphal entry.

II. Every human life is called into question by the expectation of judgment.

These warnings are difficult for many Christians today to swallow; the very idea that there are things of which God's love is not "inclusive" is regarded as an invitation to "righteous" people to demean and abuse the so-called unrighteous. As a result these harsh sayings are often passed over in silence,

11. Adolf Schlatter, *Gottes Gerechtigkeit: Ein Kommentar zum Römerbrief* (Stuttgart: Calver, 1935) 35. Schlatter, despite his criticism of the so-called Lutheran reading of Paul, is quite severe in his characterization of this move: "Although it is certainly true that God proves himself righteous through goodness and faithfulness, the statement that 'righteousness' here means faithfulness is a declaration of war on the Letter to the Romans" (ibid.).

or else applied only to faceless enemies and oppressors who somehow never turn out to be in church for the sermon. It is of course true that notions of good and evil can be used as a tool of dominance over others. It is also true, however, that not only will the all-inclusive God never sit in judgment on the marginal and unpopular; he will also never sit in judgment on *me*. If we may ask whether zeal for judgment is being used as a pretext for oppression, then surely we may ask with just as much right whether distaste for judgment is serving as a pretext for evasion.

Before the horizon of judgment we must all identify ourselves not as the judges but as those who will be judged. This is how the expectation of God's judgment, God's *final* and *definitive* judgment, clarifies and purifies our attitude to judgment. In human affairs there are inevitably judges and those who are judged, not only in courtrooms but in manifold analogical forms spread all through human society. But before the horizon of the Last Judgment, those who judge and those who are judged must stand together to await judgment, not from another human being of limited vision and imperfect character, but from the Lord God. "No creature is hidden from his sight, but all are naked and exposed to the eyes of him to whom we must give account" (Heb 4:13).

I believe that this is the real point St. Paul is making at the beginning of the second chapter of Romans. His address to "every one of you who judges" is not addressed to Jews, as though they were peculiarly "judgmental." He is not even saying that it is wrong for human beings to pass judgment on crime and wickedness—that would be very odd for him to say in light of Romans 13. He is cutting off a way of escape from his charge that human beings are "without excuse"—that they can make no defense— before God's judgment (cf. Rom 1:20; 2:1). *We cannot escape judgment by taking God's side.* We cannot insure our own righteousness by condemning the ungodly, the sexually immoral, or the oppressors of the poor, not even if we sit in judgment as God's servants, whether in the church or in the commonwealth. There will be "tribulation and distress for *every* human being who does evil . . . for God shows no partiality" (Rom 2:9, 11).

In traditional Christianity, let us be honest, it was a severe thing to live before the horizon of judgment. Those who practice awareness of judgment have to reckon with having no secrets—none at all. I can testify that when we taught together, Michael Root used to give students quite a turn by pointing out that in the Last Judgment, everything inside them, every little knot of hatred or resentment or vanity or dishonest, will be disclosed in its bare truth to the whole universe. I'm not sure, though, that it isn't more frightening to realize that in the end *I myself* will be unable to deny the truth about myself. For most of us, what we know of ourselves is a small collection of acceptable objects carefully chosen and cautiously permitted to emerge from the dim and musty basement of the heart. We have little enthusiasm for discovering what else might be lurking in there; we try to go about our business in the upstairs rooms that we have arranged to our liking and ignore the ominous noises from below.

To live before the awareness of judgment is to know that such conceal-ment will someday come to an end, that every creeping, crawling, howling thing hiding in that basement will be brought up into the light for all to see—for *me* to see. Did I really think that I could live a tidy, controlled, self-congratulatory existence upstairs without being affected by the fumes from below? Did I really believe that I had succeeded in isolating all that mess away from my attitudes and behavior?

Then too, those who live before the horizon of judgment inescap-ably find themselves asking, "Just what *concretely* does 'termination of evil' mean?" What is left behind when the "spirit of burning" has done its work? When evil is purged away from God's creation, where will *I* be? A society desperately striving to maintain self-esteem does not want to entertain such questions, but they cannot be avoided before the horizon of judgment. "Nothing unclean" will enter the promised City, "and everyone who loves and practices falsehood" will be left outside. How then can *I* go in? How can *I* enter, if others are to have peace, if there are to be no more tears?

III. There is no salvation without judgment.

The burden of living before the horizon of judgment has moved many mod-ern Christians to propose salvation without judgment. Perhaps the gospel is simply the good news that God never really was angry with sin, that God embraces us without burning, accepts us without calling us into question. This has been the message of mainline Protestantism for a long time, and in recent decades some forms of progressive Catholicism have joined in.

The problem is that salvation without judgment is not much to get excited about. Earlier Christians may well have overemphasized the thread of the *extrinsic* punishment of sin, hellfire and brimstone raining down upon the wicked. This may perhaps have encouraged both orthodox and revisionist Christians in modern times to forget that sin also involves *corruption*—rot and decay. Sin damages our humanity, prevents our flourishing, and brings us down to death. In Rom 1, God's wrath at human ungodliness is not described in terms of the violence of the Flood or the sulfur and fire raining down on Sodom. St. Paul describes a much more subtle and more terrifying display of divine anger. "Therefore God *gave them up* in the lusts of their hearts to impurity. . . . God *gave them up* to dishonorable passions . . . to a debased mind" (Rom 1:24, 26, 28).

This, I would suggest, is a foretaste of the true damnation. As long as God batters us with fire and flood, there is hope: perhaps the fire will be purifying, the flood cleansing. If or when God has had enough, though, this would be the final word: "Have it your way, then. I hand you over to the power of your desires." Then no punishment from outside would be necessary; we would be our own punishment as we spiraled down and down into disintegration and incoherence.

This is why the gospel of universal inclusivity is so profoundly sad and offers no hope to anyone. It comes to us amidst the shabbiness of our lives, the decomposition of our integrity, the shrinking of our aspirations, and tells us that God is satisfied with that, that we need not fear or feel bad as our lives decay. It is a message actively at odds with hope, because hope might make us dissatisfied with ourselves and cause us pain. It presents as Good News the thought that since there is nothing to hope for anyway, we need no longer torment ourselves with the desire of becoming different than we are.

Real salvation is bound up with judgment; *saving* love burns. Consider the repentance of King David after his murder of Uriah. The truth that the prophet Nathan sets before him is not pretty. He has murdered a loyal servant in order to take away the man's wife, and he has used the enemies of Israel to do it. God's recompense will be destructive; evil will rise up from his own house and he will be shamed before all Israel. Where does salvation lie for David in the face of this judgment?

Doubtless David could refuse judgment, perhaps execute the prophet for sedition, and resolutely continue to justify himself with lies and excuses. But what would that mean for him? It would surely mean his willful descent into what would in effect be a kind of madness—to be sure, a kind of madness so familiar that we usually consider it normal. Responding so, he would choose what was *not real*; he would reject truth.[12] He would re-

---

12. Cf. St. Athanasius, *Contra Gentes*, I, 7: When human beings turned from God, they "began to devise and imagine for themselves *what was not*, after their own pleasure"

double his disrespect for the Lord's word, which he would only be able to experience thereafter as a mortal threat to his chosen unreality. In Psalm 51, the repentant David prays, "Cast me not away from your presence, and take not your Holy Spirit from me" (v. 11). A David who refused judgment would cast *himself* away from God's presence, for God is light and no lie can survive before him. "And this is the judgment: the light has come into the world, and people loved the darkness better than the light, because their deeds were evil" (John 3:19).

The other possible course is the one David actually follows. *He yields to truth.* He consents to the judgment pronounced by the prophet. His only words are terse, without excuse: "I have sinned against the Lord" (v. 13). He accepts and acknowledges the demolition by God's word of judgment of whatever fantasies he has woven around his actions. Nor does he expect his confession to gain him immunity from the shame and loss that sin entails. His public fasting and pleading in prayer constitute an acknowledgment of his shame, an assumption of responsibility for the harm he has done.

The murder of Uriah is a strange moment in the story of David. It is as though the rising young man who would not harm Saul, who protected Saul's son, who thought so little of his own dignity that he danced naked before the ark of the Lord, has been replaced by a stranger, a cold and ego-centric tyrant. We know how that goes, when people come into power. But in the final chapters of the story, the declining king who weeps and laments for the son who tried to destroy him seems like an older and sadder version of that earlier David. In between is the judgment of God pronounced by Nathan and David's submission to that judgment. The judgment rights the balance so far as possible between David and Uriah; at least Uriah's murderer is called to account. But the judgment also delivers *David* from whatever it was that was growing in him and disclosed itself in adultery and murder. The bloodstains are cleansed from David "by a spirit of *mishpat* and a spirit of burning."

I have said that I will not address the problem of universalism in this lecture, but I will say something about a particular universalist. A friend of mine remarked to me years ago that the Scottish writer George MacDonald, who had such an influence on C. S. Lewis, made universalism a harsh and dreadful doctrine. In MacDonald's universalism, the God of implacable love will track you down and take you in hand and you will burn in his grip until every hint of evil is gone from you. What I want to commend

---

(my emphasis).

in MacDonald is not his universalism but the clarity of his perception that *salvation comes through judgment*:

> For, when we say that God is Love, do we teach men that their fear of him is groundless? No. As much as they fear will come upon them, possibly far more. . . . The wrath will consume what they *call* themselves; so that the selves God made shall appear.[13]

Nothing unclean will enter into the blessed City, for if it contained uncleanness it would not be finally and unconditionally blessed. Nothing unclean will remain in the blessed of God, for if they were marred by uncleanness they would not be finally and unconditionally blessed.

IV. It is in Jesus Christ that God's judgment is saving for us.

We find ourselves at an impasse; we can't live with God's judgment and we can't live without it. Judgment seems to bar our way into the City of God, and yet there would be no point in entering only to take uncleanness with us, only to find there a new scene in which to love and practice falsehood.

In the marvel of his grace, God has rendered his judgment on us *saving* in Jesus Christ. Christ has borne the judgment of God in our place and on our behalf, so that in him we might be judged—and saved. At least part of what it means that Jesus was judged in our place is that his death exposes the *truth* about sin. This is not so much a matter of making a public example—"See, this is what sinners deserve"—as it is the acknowledgment of sin's truth *by the one who acts for us*, the one who takes responsibility for us as our King and Lord. "The one who knew no sin was made sin for us, so that in him we might become the righteousness of God" (2 Cor 5:21).

The abandonment of Christ on the cross is our Lord's human experience of the true horror of sin. As Pope John Paul II wrote,

> Jesus' cry on the Cross, dear Brothers and Sisters, is not the cry of anguish of a man without hope, but the prayer of the Son who offers his life to the Father in love, for the salvation of all. At the very moment when he identifies with our sin, "abandoned" by the Father, he "abandons" himself into the hands of the Father. His eyes remain fixed on the Father. Precisely because of the

---

13. George MacDonald, "The Consuming Fire," in *Unspoken Sermons, Series I, II and III*, Facsimile Reprint Edition (Whitethorn, CA: Johannesen, 1978) 29.

> knowledge and experience of the Father which he alone has, even
> at this moment of darkness he sees clearly the gravity of sin and
> suffers because of it. He alone, who sees the Father and rejoices
> fully in him, can understand completely what it means to resist the
> Father's love by sin.[14]

In Christ, then, things are put right between God and humankind, in the first
place because the truth is exposed definitively by God's act of judgment. And
at the same time, the relationship between God and humankind is founded
anew on the basis of Christ's love and obedience, offered on our behalf.

This has not happened so that we may escape judgment, but rather so
that we may experience judgment as salvation in him. When we are joined
to Christ by the Spirit through faith, his life becomes our life. Insofar as
we are united with him, we are no longer simply identified with our own
sinfulness. The fire can burn and consume the evil in us, and there will still
be something left—the self-in-Christ, the new self. Faith in Christ divides
us and sets us at odds with ourselves; the desires of the flesh conflict with
the desires of the Spirit, but now I am not simply identical with my flesh
and its desires, for "those who belong to Christ have crucified the flesh with
its passions and desires" (Gal 5:24).

At the same time, to be joined to be Christ is to be joined to *truth*. If
he lives in us, then his *truthfulness* lives in us as penitence, as submission
to judgment. The nineteenth-century Lutheran theologian Adolf von Harless described the relationship of union with Christ to the repentance of
Christians in this way:

> Christ is essentially our peace and the prince of peace, that is, the
> one who dissolves the rupture between God and humankind. But
> he does not do this in such a way as to deny the rupture, rather
> he confirms it. He does not liberate us from the accusations of
> conscience and the verdict of the law by denying their truth and
> justice; he affirms both, in that he endures in our place the verdict
> of the law and accomplishes the victory of God's mercy over the
> just verdict. It is this that he wants to bring into our inner experi-
> ence through the work of the Holy Spirit.[15]

When we are joined to Christ by faith, therefore, we are joined to the truth,
and the truth lives and works in us. The truthfulness of Christ takes shape

---

14. Pope John Paul II, Apostolic Letter *Novo Millennia Ineunte*, 65.

15. Gottlieb Christoph Adolf von Harless, *Christliche Ethik* (Stuttgart: Sam. Gottl.
Lisching, 1842) 242.

within us as our continual and ever-deepening repentance, in which we come to know the reality of our sin more and more clearly and more and more come to hate it. This penitent knowledge will be perfected in us on the Last Day, when the Lord brings to light things now hidden in darkness and discloses the purposes of the heart (1 Cor 4:5).

Because the Christian life is a life in *Christ* it has, in the meantime, the irreducible structure of dying and living, judgment and renewal, repentance and sanctification, always together, never separated. To be saved is to live under judgment, to acknowledge judgment, to endure judgment—but *in Christ*, in union with the one who gives us himself as our life in exchange for all that judgment takes away. To be saved is to expect judgment, and to be free to welcome it, because it can take away nothing that we need if we are in Christ.

To live before the horizon of judgment is to live in a much more *serious* world than most of us educated, middle-class Christians of the early-twenty-first century find it easy to contemplate. We are aware of the terrors with which those who lived or still live in that world were and are afflicted, and it is no surprise that we are not eager to submit ourselves to them. But our reluctance, however understandable, has no bearing on the question of the *truth* of the scriptural proclamation of judgment. I wonder moreover if there were and are not compensations for those terrors. In a life lived before the horizon of judgment, I wonder whether the gospel of Christ might bring keener joys, more audacious hopes, and the gift of a greater dignity than most of us can imagine.

2

Why Hell Still Burns

Jerry Walls

WEEKS BEFORE ROB BELL'S 2011 book *Love Wins: A Book about Heaven, Hell and the Fate of Every Person Who Ever Lived*[1] was published, it ignited a firestorm of controversy on the Internet, due largely to rumors that the book affirmed universal salvation, the notion that all persons will eventually be saved. When the book finally appeared the flames of controversy spread to such an extent that the cover of *Time* magazine posed the question that Christians throughout America were asking afresh: "What if there's no hell?"[2]

As this episode vividly demonstrates, the suggestion that there's no hell is still loaded enough to stir the passions of many American Christians in the early twenty-first century. It is worth pausing, however, to reflect that things were rather different not so very long before. Less than three decades earlier, in 1985, Martin Marty published an article with the telling title, "Hell Disappeared. No One Noticed. A Civic Argument." What is striking here is Marty's argument that hell had, for all practical purposes, become "culturally unavailable" in the sense that no one really took it seriously

---

1. Rob Bell, *Love Wins: A Book about Heaven, Hell and the Fate of Every Person Who Ever Lived* (New York: HarperOne, 2011).

2. April 25, 2011.

anymore. In support of his claim, he noted that a bibliographical search for contemporary literature on hell turned up almost nothing on the subject.[3] Four years later, in 1989, Harvard theologian Gordon Kaufman, citing what he saw as "irreversible changes," pronounced: "I don't think there can be any future for heaven and hell."[4]

Within the circles of university divinity schools, it appeared the flames of hell had been reduced to a flicker and would soon die out. In retrospect, it is easy to see how wildly misguided was Kaufman's prediction, and indeed, it is tempting to comment that his prediction also shows how far out of touch with the world of true believers are theologians whose primary gauge of reality is the American Academy of Religion. For anyone who was paying attention was aware that America in the 1980s was in the midst of a revival of evangelical Christianity, on the heels of 1976 (the year Jimmy Carter was elected president) being hailed as "the year of the evangelical." And anyone who is even remotely familiar with evangelical Christianity knows it aspires to take the Bible seriously. At the heart of evangelical Christianity is the conviction that it is essential to have personal faith in Jesus in order to be saved. Without such personal faith, one is hopelessly lost. The urgency that one's eternal fate is at stake has always deeply informed evangelical piety and missions.

This, in brief, is a large part of the explanation for why hell still burns. It is an integral component of the web of beliefs I just sketched, and as long as those beliefs have credibility for significant numbers of people, hell is not likely to lack a future. Indeed, just two years after Kaufman's pronouncement, the cover of *U.S. News and World Report* announced "The Rekindling of Hell" with "Hell" in large red letters. The story inside, titled "Hell's Sober Comeback," reported that "hell is undergoing something of a revival in American religious thought," even among theologians.[5] The next year, Zondervan published the volume *Four Views of Hell*,[6] providing further evidence that the debate had indeed been rekindled, and the same year, Notre Dame published my book *Hell: The Logic of Damnation*, in which I offered a philosophical defense of eternal hell. The following year yet an-

3. Martin E. Marty, "Hell Disappeared. No One Noticed. A Civic Argument," *Harvard Theological Review* 78 (1985) 393.

4. Cited by Kenneth L. Woodward, "Heaven," *Newsweek*, March 27, 1989, 54.

5. "Hell's Sober Comeback," *U.S. News and World Report*, March 25, 1991, 56. Nine years later, hell was the cover story of the same magazine. See Jeffery L. Sheler, "Hell Hath No Fury," *U.S. News and World Report*, January 31, 2000.

6. William Crockett, ed. *Four Views of Hell* (Grand Rapids: Zondervan, 1992).

other philosophical defense of hell by Jonathan Kvanvig was published by Oxford University Press.[7] It is safe to say that by this point, the issue was squarely back on the table, and anyone who has been following the matter knows it has been a subject of lively debate among Christian philosophers and theologians ever since.

The Appeal to Scripture and the Broader Issues

In the space that remains, I want to look at some of the issues in the current debate, beginning with claim that Scripture requires us to accept the doctrine of eternal hell, a claim that has been the trump card for most believers in the traditional doctrine. The appeal to Scripture on this point is often thought to have particular force since Christ himself is the speaker in many of the key texts cited to prove the doctrine. But one of the fascinating things about the current debate is that critics of the doctrine of eternal hell have seized the mantle of biblical authority with no less zeal than its defenders. In particular, this is true of advocates of universal salvation, as well as proponents of annihilation for the lost. While defenders of eternal hell have always been confident that Scripture squarely supports their view, it may be a little more surprising that advocates of universalism and annihilationism claim the biblical high ground no less fervently, if not stridently, than their more traditional opponents.

This was well illustrated in a book several years ago titled *Two Views of Hell: A Biblical and Theological Dialogue,* in which Edward Fudge made the case for annihilationism and Robert A. Peterson argued for the more traditional view of hell as eternal misery. In the introduction, the authors cited the text in Matthew 25 pertaining to the final fate of the lost, and then commented, "There is no need to quote multiple passages; universalism is incompatible with clear biblical teaching."[8]

While theological issues came into the debate at certain points, the dialogue centered almost entirely around the authors' divergent interpretations of a number of key biblical texts that describe the fate of the lost, including the one in Matthew 25. But what was particularly striking was that each of them at numerous points insisted that Scripture clearly taught his view as clearly as it rules out universalism. For a couple notable instances,

7. Jonathan L. Kvanvig, *The Problem of Hell* (Oxford: Oxford University Press, 1993).

8. Edward William Fudge and Robert A. Peterson, *Two Views of Hell: A Biblical and Theological Dialogue* (Downers Grove, IL: InterVarsity, 2000) 14.

Fudge, after spelling out his interpretation of various sayings of Jesus, declared, "Jesus could not say it any more plainly."[9] And in commenting on 2 Pet 2:6, he writes, "If Peter could hear the conversation, he would probably scratch his head and wonder how he could have possibly written more plainly."[10] In response, Peterson chides Fudge for claiming that Scripture is "crystal clear" in teaching annihilation, but then makes similar claims for his own views. For instance, in commenting on Matt 25:41 and Rev 20:10, he writes that "the conclusion is irresistible" that those who are unsaved "will suffer eternal conscious torment."[11]

Now to give the debate even more spice, the same sort of confident claims are also advanced on behalf of universalism by some of its adherents. Many who could be classified as universalists are only what I would call "hopeful universalists" because they hold the relatively uncontroversial position that it is permissible at least to hope for universal salvation, if not the slightly stronger claim that we *should* hope for it. To hope for something, implies, of course, that one believes it is at least possible, if not somewhat probable. Moreover, if universal salvation is possible, this implies that either it is possible that everyone dies in a state of grace (contrary to appearances) or that postmortem conversion is possible. As I understand it, Roman Catholic theology forbids teaching universal salvation, but does permit hoping and praying for it, so presumably Roman Catholic theology affirms either that it is possible that all die in a state of grace, or that postmortem conversion is possible.

A number of Protestant philosophers and theologians have taken a stronger stance with regard to universal salvation, and have affirmed it as a certainty. A particularly interesting example is Thomas Talbott, who has argued that is not merely possible that universalism is true, and therefore a viable thing to hope for, but rather, it is the only position that is even possibly true. We will examine his philosophical argument for this below, but for now it should come as no surprise that he thinks Scripture is utterly clear in teaching that all will in fact be saved. And so, his exegetical defense of universalism is sprinkled with remarks like his claim that Paul's parallel statement on the two Adams in Rom 5:18 "eliminate[s] any possibility of ambiguity." And he

9. Ibid., 50.
10. Ibid., 200.
11. Ibid., 107.

follows this up a few lines later by reiterating, "Again, I do not know how Paul could have expressed himself any more clearly than that."[12]

Now, dare I say it, these conflicting claims "clearly" pose serious problems, at least for anyone who believes Scripture is the word of God, and is logically consistent in its doctrinal and moral teachings. And it is surely beyond dispute that the claim that all persons will be saved is incompatible with the claim that some persons will be eternally lost, either by remaining separated from God forever in hell, or by being annihilated in the end. Both cannot be true. Likewise, the claim that all persons who are finally lost will be annihilated is starkly incompatible with the claim that all the lost will remain consciously alive in hell forever. (One could, however, consistently hold that some will be annihilated and some will remain forever separated from God.) So all three claims about the final outcome of things cannot be true, and indeed, only one can be.

Nevertheless, the fact that the three claims are mutually incompatible does not necessarily entail that any of them are false interpretations of Scripture. Perhaps all three of contestants cited above are correct in their claims about what Scripture clearly and obviously teaches. Taking this line, however, leads to the rather puzzling conclusion that Scripture teaches irreconcilably inconsistent things about hell. If so, anyone who believes Scripture is the word of God would have to conclude that it does not reveal to us which of the three mutually exclusive claims are true. Indeed, perhaps the fact that Scripture "clearly" teaches three mutually incompatible claims is meant to suggest that God does not want us to know the truth of this matter and that the truth of the matter must remain opaque until the end of the world. Those with a fondness for paradox and/or those attracted to apophatic theology may welcome this conclusion.

But unless one is prepared to embrace something like this, the claim that Scripture clearly teaches all three, or even two of the three, mutually inconsistent views is rather implausible. So as a defender of the doctrine of eternal hell, I am prepared to acknowledge that there are texts that teach this doctrine alongside other texts that appear to teach universalism and still others that appear to teach annihilationism. Notice: Scripture in places *appears* to teach annihilationism just as it *appears* in still other places to teach universalism. In putting it this way, I mean to say that I believe Scripture does reveal the truth to us in this disputed matter, but I do not

---

12. Thomas Talbott, "Christ Victorious," in *Universal Salvation? The Current Debate*, edite by Robin Parry and Chris Partridge (Carlisle: Paternoster, 2003) 19.

believe it is as "crystal clear" as a number of the various disputants in this matter think it is. I am of course, not an exegete, and perhaps if I were, I would have stronger convictions about what the text clearly teaches. But as a philosopher involved in the debate, I remain dubious of these mutually exclusive claims to undeniable clarity.

Now then, does this simply leave us at an impasse? While this is a tempting conclusion, I would argue that there is relative clarity in another direction. In particular, I would argue that it is clear that the burden of proof lies heavily with universalists and annihilationists, and unless one of those two positions can muster an exegetical case that becomes widely persuasive, then it is reasonable for defenders of eternal hell to continue to insist that Scripture supports their view. For whereas the exegetical evidence may be far from decisive, what is much more clear is that there is a broad and overwhelming consensus in historical theology that some will be lost, and that they will remain forever in conscious misery, at the very least, that this is possible.

I hasten to add that the point here is not simply an appeal to tradition, but rather, a point about what is involved in holding that Scripture does in fact reveal the truth on this matter rather than intentionally leaving us with an unbreakable deadlock. For the word "reveal" is a classic instance of an achievement verb. If something is revealed, the recipients of the revelation must have understood the essential message correctly, otherwise revelation does not succeed, but fails. Now the fact that there is such an overwhelming consensus in favor of eternal conscious hell is rather impressive prima facie evidence that God did not intend us to read the text as teaching either universalism or annihilationism.

I emphasize that this is only *prima facie* evidence, though I think it is fairly weighty and could not easily be overturned. Universalists will rightly point out that there is a stream of support for universalism throughout Church history, starting with Origen and Gregory of Nyssa. However, after those early towering figures, support for universalism waned considerably, and many of its defenders, including Origen himself, were of dubious orthodoxy, and their universalism was often motivated by fanciful metaphysical schemes.[13] On this score, moreover, annihilationism faces an even

13. For an informative survey, see Morwenna Ludlow, *Universal Salvation?* (Oxford: Oxford University Press, 2009) 191–218.

heavier burden of proof, for it cannot claim even as much of a theological legacy as universalism.[14]

As the debate moves forward, I believe it will be essential to expand the discussion beyond those relatively few texts which deal directly with hell and focus on the larger biblical narrative as well as broader theological and philosophical issues, and how these bear on our interpretation of the controversial texts. In the brief space that remains, I will mention three such issues: the aesthetic/theodicy issue; the perfect happiness issue; and the freedom issue. In identifying these as theological/philosophical issues, I do not mean that these are non-biblical issues, but only to emphasize that our stance on these questions will very much affect how we interpret the texts that directly address hell as a possible human destiny.

Let us begin with the aesthetic/theodicy issue. As Talbott notes, both universalists and annihilationists believe that God will completely and utterly destroy sin and evil in the end when all things are made new. By contrast, he claims, those who believe in eternal hell believe that God merely quarantines evil and sin.[15] If so, God's victory over evil would arguably be less complete, for his world would still be marred by the presence of evil, even if the scales of justice are balanced in hell.

Now I am willing to concede that the universalist story gives us the most beautiful, the most satisfying ending of the human story, and would allow us to celebrate that drama as an unqualified comedy in the most glorious sense of that word. In this regard, it also trumps the annihilationist account, for in their picture, some lives end in the ultimate tragedy of total destruction. While all evil may appear to be destroyed on the annihilationist account, there is still one glaring exception, namely, the sad memories of those who would be lost forever. The memories of loved ones who resisted God until the end and were finally destroyed would linger as a lasting evil.

This brings us to the perfect happiness issue, which was formulated by the nineteenth-century theologian Friedrich Schleiermacher. The essence of his argument was that if any persons are lost forever in hell, then the happiness of heaven could not be perfect, because the misery of those in hell would cast a shadow over the happiness of the blessed. It is easy to see his point if one thinks of persons in heaven who may have loved ones in

14 Glenn Peoples has convinced me that there is more evidence for conditional immortality in the fathers than I previously realized. See his essay at this site: http://www.afterlife.co.nz/2013/theology/history-of-hell/.

15. Talbott, "Christ Victorious," 22, 28.

hell. Could one be perfectly happy if, say, one's beloved wife, mother, or child was in hell? While this makes the point more vivid, it does not depend on such personal relationships. Indeed, it can be argued that all those in heaven, starting with God, are filled with perfect love and, consequently, would grieve the misery of any lost sheep regardless of whether they had been personally related to them in this life.

Now it is worth noting that this problem was not felt by many classical theologians. To the contrary, such notable proponents of eternal hell as Augustine, Aquinas, and Jonathan Edwards held that the justice served on the inhabitants of hell, and their consequent misery, would actually enhance the pleasure of the redeemed. To make matters worse, Augustine, Edwards, and perhaps Aquinas (though this is debated by Thomists) were theological determinists, so the denizens of hell are punished forever for sins that God himself determined them to commit.

The problem that Schleiermacher identified is one that many contemporary believers will keenly feel. The problem is perhaps seen in its sharpest light in view of one of the most appealing promises about heaven, namely, that God will wipe every tear from our eyes.[16] The specter of being haunted by grief over the lost makes it hard to see how this could be true. Moreover, this is also a problem for annihilationists, as I have already noted. Even if hell does not persist as an ongoing reality, the memory of loved ones finally destroyed threatens to cast shadows over the perfect joy of heaven just as eternal hell does. There have been various suggested solutions to this problem, and I have defended one of them,[17] but for now I have the space simply to record that I do not find any of them fully satisfying. So again, I will concede that universalism can avoid a difficulty that afflicts both annihilationism and the doctrine of eternal hell.

Thirdly, we come to the issue of freedom. Here I begin with the widely shared judgment that if we are not free in the libertarian sense, we have virtually no chance of making sense of the problem of evil. Both eternal hell and annihilationism exacerbate the difficulties already posed by the problem of evil, and indeed, I have argued elsewhere that any such doctrine is utterly indefensible if we do not have libertarian freedom. Both eternal

16. As Talbott points out, this argument is usually cast as a philosophical argument, but it has biblical roots, such as Paul's statement that he would be cursed if he could save his countrymen. See "Christ Victorious," 15–18.

17. Jerry L. Walls, *Hell: The Logic of Damnation* (Notre Dame: University of Notre Dame Press, 1992) 106–10.

hell and annihilationism are deeply incompatible with the claim that God is good, let alone perfectly good, if all our choices are determined.[18]

Now here is where Talbott's necessary universalism runs into severe difficulty and loses whatever advantages it may have gained on the previous two points. For if we are truly free in the libertarian sense, it seems mostly likely that if we can resist and reject God and his love in this life, as it seems many people are doing, then we can go on rejecting him, even forever. And if so, it is possible, if not likely, that some will be forever lost in a hell they have constructed through their own ongoing choice to refuse the love of God. C. S. Lewis captured the essence of this idea when he wrote, "I willingly believe that the damned are, in one sense, successful, rebels to the end; that the doors of hell are locked on the *inside*."[19]

The suggestion that the persisting choice to lock God out is the reason why hell is eternal is a very different explanation for the eternity of hell than that of most classical theologians. The predominant argument in classical theology is based on divine justice and the claim that eternal punishment is the just sentence for human sin. One variation of this for instance, holds that any sin against an infinitely good God deserves infinite punishment. So any sin that is not atoned for must be receive infinite punishment if God is to be just. A number of critics, however, have raised what is known as the "proportionality problem," which contends that there is a radical disproportion between any sin finite beings could commit and infinite punishment.

The appeal to human freedom, then, is a way to undercut this objection, since eternal hell is not defended on the grounds only of sins committed in this life. Rather, it is the persistence of sin, the ongoing rejection of God and his grace that keeps hell going forever. Given the importance of the appeal to human freedom in the current debate, let us examine this more carefully.

Can Freedom Block Universal Salvation?

I want to discuss Talbott's argument for necessary universalism in some detail, since I think it is the most interesting and most developed argument for that conclusion. However, before doing so, I want to consider more briefly another argument for universalism that aims to undercut the appeal to

18. See my essay "Why No Classical Theist, Let Alone Orthodox Christian, Should *Ever* Be a Compatibilist," *Philosophia Christi* 13 (2011) 75–104.

19. C. S. Lewis, *The Problem of Pain* (San Francisco: HarperSanFrancisco, 2001) 130.

human freedom, namely, that of Marilyn Adams. Adams has argued that this appeal is deeply misguided since it exaggerates the dignity of human nature to the level of something so sacrosanct that not even God may legitimately interfere with it. She sees this tendency particularly in those versions of the doctrine that hold hell as simply the inevitable and altogether natural consequence of freely choosing to reject a relationship with God and the love that he offers. Adams protests that advocates of this view tend to place God and humans on the same level as if they were moral peers. As she sees it, for God to give us the freedom to reject him and choose evil instead is hardly the appropriate sort of respect for him to pay to the likes of us.

Indeed, the deeper difficulty here is that free will approaches underestimate what she calls the "size gap" between Divine and created persons. Whereas free will approaches picture the relationship between God and human persons with the analogy of parents and adolescent or adult children, Adams thinks it is better modeled by the relationship between a mother and an infant or a toddler. In the latter relationship, there is little if any sense that the child is free and responsible and that it would be wrong to interfere with his choices. This nicely serves Adams's view that God can save everyone in the end, and relieves her of the worry of how God can accomplish this without violating our freedom. If God needs to causally determine some things in order to prevent the everlasting ruin of some of his children, Adams colorfully comments, this is "no more an insult to our dignity than a mother's changing a diaper is to the baby."[20]

While Adams is willing to dispense with human freedom if it stands in the way of universal salvation, Talbott wants to resist this conclusion. His philosophical case against eternal hell affirms human freedom, but argues that freedom is no barrier to universal salvation since the idea that anyone could choose eternal hell is actually incoherent when carefully examined. The fundamental reason for this is because there simply is no intelligible motive for choosing eternal hell. To be sure, one may temporarily choose evil under the illusion that so choosing will make one happy. But at the end of the day, God will eventually shatter this illusion by bringing home the consequences of choosing evil, namely, that sin will make one ever more miserable. As this realization sinks in, one will inevitably reach the point that one must repent and turn to God. Thus, Talbott affirms the view that

20. Marilyn McCord Adams, *Horrendous Evils and the Goodness of God* (Ithaca, NY: Cornell University Press, 1999) 157.

universalism is necessarily true, in contrast to the more common claims that universalism is possibly true or very probably true.

His argument for this claim hinges crucially on his account of what is involved in freely choosing an eternal destiny. In short, such a choice must be fully informed, and once the person making the choice gets what he wants, then it must be the case that he never regrets his choice. This means that the person must be free from ignorance and illusion both in his initial choice as well as later. He must fully understand what he has chosen while freely persisting in that choice.

Given these conditions, Talbott thinks there is an obvious and important asymmetry between choosing fellowship with God as an eternal destiny, on the one hand, and choosing hell as an eternal destiny, on the other. Whereas the first of these obviously is possible, the latter is not because it simply makes no sense to say someone could knowingly persist in the choice of eternal misery. In short, there is no intelligible motive for choosing eternal misery, so the idea of eternal hell is incoherent, and therefore not possibly true.

Obviously, the philosophical credibility of the doctrine of hell will largely depend on one's judgments about the nature and value of freedom as well as one's views of moral psychology. Those who disagree with Adams will argue that freedom is of sufficient value itself, or is the means to other goods of sufficient value, that God will not override it to save us. In a similar vein, to rebut Talbott's argument, we will need to make the case that there are, contrary to his claims, intelligible motives for the choice of eternal damnation. Now this is an issue that I have debated with Talbott several times over the past several years, so let us look at the controversy in more detail.

Hell Can't Last Forever?

I have already noted that Talbott's view hinges crucially on a particular view of freedom. But second, in addition to his view of what is involved in freely choosing an eternal destiny, his argument also relies heavily on his view that hell is pictured in the New Testament "as a forcibly imposed punishment rather than as a freely embraced condition."[21] This view of hell is what underwrites his claim that it is unintelligible that anyone could freely

21. Thomas B. Talbott, "Freedom, Damnation, and the Power to Sin with Impunity," *Religious Studies* 37 (2001) 417.

choose it forever. As Talbott sees it then, the forcibly imposed misery of hell will eventually move even the most recalcitrant sinners to repent and gladly and freely—in the non-determined sense—choose heaven for their eternal destiny.[22]

A third important component of his argument is a distinction he has drawn between having the power to do something, on the one hand, and being psychologically capable of doing it, on the other. As an instance of the difference, he cites Augustine's view that the redeemed in heaven will no longer even be tempted to disobey God. Indeed, they will see with such clarity that God is the source of happiness and sin is the source of misery that sin and disobedience will no longer be psychologically possible for them. But surely they will not be less free on this account Talbott points out, nor will it be the case that they lack the power to sin. Nevertheless, sin will remain a psychological impossibility for them.[23]

I accept Talbott's distinction between power and psychological ability as a helpful one. However, even with this distinction granted, there are serious problems with his claim that persons who repent under forcibly imposed punishment are free in a non-determined sense. In the first place, the notion of ever increasing misery, misery without a distinct limit, destroys the very notion of a free choice. The reason for this is that finite beings like ourselves are simply not constituted in such a way that we can absorb ever-increasing misery.

Imagine a man who is on the rack being tortured, with his tormentor continually tightening the screws. No finite person could bear such an ever-increasing amount of pain and misery. At some point, he would either be coerced to submit, or he would go insane, or he would perish. Finite beings such as we are have neither the *power* nor the *psychological ability* to withstand constantly increasing misery, regardless of whether that misery is physical or emotional in nature. Our freedom, in other words, can only take so much pressure. Where exactly the limit lies is perhaps not easy to say, but clearly there is such a limit.

For punishment to elicit a free choice that is morally significant, on the other hand, the person receiving the punishment must have the capacity to come to see the truth about himself and his actions and genuinely

22. Talbott affirms the libertarian sense of freedom in the sense that he believes "creaturely freedom could never exist in a fully determined universe." Ibid., 426.

23. Thomas B. Talbott, "On the Divine Nature and the Nature of Divine Freedom," *Faith and Philosophy* 5 (1988) 13.

want to change. He must achieve genuine moral insight in the process and sincerely desire to act on the truth that he has come to see. He must want to change because of the moral insight he has gained, not merely to avoid or blunt the pain that is being forced upon him. In short, the insight and understanding that truly transforms cannot be coerced or instilled merely by forcibly imposed punishment.

Interestingly, Talbott apparently recognizes this point. He draws a distinction between two kinds of compulsion and defends what he calls the "right" kind of compulsion, namely, that which comes from dramatic conversions that are fairly common in the Christian tradition. Many Christians have powerful experiences of God that they describe in terms that are similar to Paul's Damascus Road experience. In such encounters with God, many people feel as if they had no choice but to submit.

By contrast, Talbott repudiates the sort of compulsion that unfortunately has sometimes been employed by Christians, namely, that of demanding conversion under the threat of lethal force. He writes, "A stunning revelation such as Paul reportedly received, one that provides clear vision and *compelling evidence*, thereby altering one's beliefs in a perfectly rational way, does not compel behavior in the same way that threatening someone with a sword might."[24] Now Talbott is surely right that there is an important difference between these two kinds of compulsion, and that the latter is not only morally objectionable but also incompatible with any meaningful sense of freedom.

However, this distinction, while a helpful one, actually poses problems for Talbott, given his view of hell as "forcibly imposed punishment," or as he also puts it, "unbearable suffering."[25] For it is undeniable that the traditional accounts of hell that Talbott has endorsed surely include physical pain, and indeed, pain of a rather intense variety. If he does not believe hell includes physical pain and punishment, then he should not pretend to endorse the traditional understanding of what makes the punishment of hell unbearable.[26] However, if he does mean to endorse the traditional view, then to avoid outright inconsistency here, he owes us some explanation of

---

24. Talbott, "Freedom, Damnation, and the Power to Sin with Impunity," 427.

25. Ibid., 417.

26. In "Replies to My Critics" (*Universal Salvation? The Current Debate*) Talbott says the source of misery in hell is nothing "other than the sin that lies within" and admits that his use of the phrase "forcibly imposed punishment" is misleading if it is taken to mean more than this.

how forcibly imposed punishment that produces unbearable misery is not the wrong kind of compulsion that he expressly repudiates.

Now it is worth emphasizing that this point holds even if Talbott thinks the misery of hell is purely psychological or spiritual. If it is objectionable to compel repentance by the sword, it is likewise objectionable to compel repentance by forcibly imposed misery, whether physical, psychological, or spiritual. I take it Talbott would not want to endorse, say, a spiritual version of waterboarding as a means to induce repentance.

But there is another problem with Talbott's account of the right kind of compulsion. Notice his italicized words, namely, his appeal to "compelling evidence" that alters one's beliefs in a perfectly rational way. Now I have no problem with the idea that evidence that is taken to be compelling can alter one's beliefs in a completely rational way. Indeed, it is arguably the very nature of rationality to be willing to alter one's beliefs in light of appropriate evidence, especially if that evidence is staring one directly in the face.

I am more dubious, however, about the notion that evidence can ever truly be compelling, especially when we are dealing with matters as contested as religious truth claims. And we need not resort to anything as radical as Cartesian skepticism, or the elaborately sophisticated arguments that philosophers can generate to defend almost any position. Rather, we simply need to recognize that there is more to belief than the intellect assessing evidence. The will is also involved, and if our disposition is adverse, the evidence will hardly compel us. Pascal commented extensively on the role of the heart and other aspects of our person when it comes to belief. Here is one of his telling observations along these lines: "Contradiction is a poor indication of truth. Many things that are certain are contradicted. Many that are false pass without contradiction. Contradiction is no more an indication of falsehood than lack of it is an indication of truth."[27]

This is not to deny that there is good evidence in favor of belief. But there is a vast difference between adequate evidence and compelling evidence. Indeed, it is arguable that the evidence needs to be at least adequate for belief to be rational, but short of compelling, for us to be properly free in our response to it. Certainly Pascal thought it was important that the evidence for Christianity be at least as good as the evidence against it, for if it were not then it would arguably be irrational to believe. Such belief would have to be an act of the will to fly in the face of the evidence, a view

27. Blaise Pascal, *Pensees*, translated by A. J. Krailsheimer (London: Penguin, 1966) no. 177.

that Pascal rejects. But again, it is at least equally important to be clear that faith is also very much a matter of the heart. That is, it is a matter of having one's heart rightly disposed, of loving the right things for the right reasons, and so on.

This insight is also relevant to another major theme in Pascal's thought, namely his explanation of the hiddenness of God. God is hidden because he has no interest in merely satisfying our intellectual curiosity. Because he is hidden, we must seriously seek him in response to his prompting, and as we do so, he reveals himself to us more and more. But his self-disclosure varies according to our willingness to open our hearts to the truth and follow it.[28]

This brings us back to the point that evidence can never be compelling, strictly speaking. If our hearts are not open to accept and follow the truth, we can contradict even that which is certain, as Pascal observed. To be sure, we can be confident that a perfectly good God will reveal himself and his truth to us with sufficient clarity to make clear the disposition of our hearts. In this sense the evidence is indeed compelling, but there is no certainty that when the dispositions of our hearts are revealed that we will embrace and follow the truth.

Unfortunately for Talbott then, neither "compelling evidence" nor "unbearable suffering" can guarantee the sort of free response that God desires from his creatures. Evidence can never be compelling in the relevant sense, and unbearable suffering cannot elicit a response that is truly morally free. A response that is extracted by unbearable suffering is compelled in a sense that destroys any meaningful sense of freedom.

But What about the Rich Man and Lazarus?

Let's continue to explore these points in light of a famous biblical account of hell, namely, the story of the rich man and Lazarus. This story is relevant to our discussion in the first place because Talbott cites as evidence for the view that hell is forcibly imposed punishment.[29] It is also interesting from another angle, however, since I have often heard it cited against the idea of postmortem repentance. That is to say, it is alleged that the story shows the rich man sincerely repenting, but his repentance is rejected because it is too late. This shows, moreover, so the argument goes, that hell is not eternal because of the

28. For more on this, see Thomas V. Morris, *Making Sense of It All: Pascal and the Meaning of Life* (Grand Rapids: Eerdmans, 1992).

29. Talbott, "Freedom, Damnation, and the Power to Sin with Impunity," 417.

ongoing refusal to repent by its denizens, but rather because they are receiving their just desserts for their sins in this life. Hell is eternal not because the doors or hell are locked on the inside, as Lewis would have it, but instead because its inhabitants are forced to stay there against their wishes, even though they would gladly repent and receive salvation if they could.

Now it is worth noting that this story may be a parable, but whether it is or not, we cannot press all the details of the story and assume each of them is intended to make a specific point. However, I believe there are other viable interpretations of it that support neither Talbott's view of hell, nor the view that the inhabitants of hell are forced to stay there despite their sincere repentance.

First, there is nothing in the story to indicate the misery of the rich man was an unbearable punishment that led to his repentance and eventual salvation. That is precisely the scenario we would expect if Talbott's theory of hell is correct. Contrary to this, the "great gulf" that separates the rich man from Lazarus remains between them, without any indication that it will be traversed.

Second, despite the rich man's misery he seems more concerned to justify himself than to truly repent and sincerely throw himself on God's mercy. Although his first request is for relief from his pain, his next request is for Lazarus to be sent to his brothers to warn them so they can escape his fate. While this appears on the surface to be a loving gesture on behalf of his brothers, it may equally well be understood as an indirect attempt at self-justification. The implied suggestion in this request is that if he had been better informed and warned, *he would not be there either.* Indeed, his demand is arguably for compelling evidence, the very sort of thing that Talbott thinks would be convincing and move all sinners to repentance.

But third, notice that his suggestion is countered by Abraham's response when he points out that his brothers have Moses and the prophets. When the rich man retorts that more is needed, that they would repent if someone from the dead went to them, Abraham rejects this out of hand: "If they do not listen to Moses and the Prophets, they will not be convinced even if someone rises from the dead" (Luke 16:31). The point seems clear that the rich man is not in hell because he lacked sufficient evidence. Just like his brothers, he had available to him Moses and the Prophets. And Moses and the Prophets warned against indifference to the poor, yet the rich man ignored Lazarus as he lay at his gate covered with sores. In other words, he had more than enough evidence but declined to act on the truth that was clearly in front of him.

As I see it then, hell is indeed a place of misery but not unbearable misery. This is why it can be freely chosen forever as one's eternal destiny. Still, there is something deeply puzzling, if not paradoxical about this, and Talbott certainly raises an obvious question in asking what possible motive could explain such a choice. Indeed, I would grant that the choice of hell is deeply irrational, and we cannot make full sense of it. Nevertheless, it does have its own sort of logic, and we can make coherent sense of it.

The nature and dynamics of this choice has been depicted with striking psychological plausibility by the characters C. S. Lewis portrays in his little theological fantasy, *The Great Divorce*. The premise of the book, of course, is that a group of "ghosts" from hell take a bus ride to heaven, and are invited, indeed, implored to leave their sins behind and stay. The stunning thing is that almost all of them choose to return to hell.

One of the most memorable characters is the aggrieved "Big Ghost," who has come to heaven with the goal of getting his rights. One of his former employees, who was a murderer, is in heaven, and this man is his heavenly host who has been sent to meet him and tell him what he needs to do to stay there himself. He is most insulted by this arrangement, and believes their roles should have been reversed. He should be in heaven, he thinks, and the murderer in hell. What he cannot fathom is that he too, like the murderer, is a sinner who needs forgiveness and transformation. He insists he has always done his best, and has no need of "charity." When the terms are laid down that he cannot make it to heaven without help, and he must receive it from his former employee, he chooses to return to hell: "'Tell them I'm not coming, see? I'd rather be damned than to go along with you. I came here to get my rights, see? Not to go sniveling along on charity tied to your apron strings. If they are too fine to have me without you, I'll go home.' It was almost happy now that it could, in a sense, threaten."[30] The telling phrase here is the one that describes the Big Ghost as "almost happy now that it could, in a sense, threaten." And this is the essential insight that makes intelligible the choice of hell. While there is not a shred of true joy or real happiness in hell, it does offer its substitutes for the real thing. The Big Ghost does not have real power, only a shadowy illusion of power in his effort to threaten. Bitterness and resentment have their pleasures, as does an aggrieved sense of self-righteousness. Again, this pleasure is a tawdry substitute for the real item, but the point remains

30. C. S. Lewis, *The Great Divorce* (San Francisco: HarperSanFrancisco, 2001) 31.

that there is a certain perverse sense of pleasure in these hellish imitations of true happiness and this makes intelligible the choice of eternal hell.

Furthermore, it is a clear moral and spiritual truth that repentance and transformation involve a certain amount of discomfort and even pain. To give up the resentment and self-righteousness that keep us from true happiness is not easy, and the more we have invested, the more difficult it may be. Faced with the painful choices that transformation requires, it is intelligible that some could prefer to hold on to their sins and the distorted pleasures they afford rather than submit to the painful process of transformation. This preference is another part of the complex motivational structure that makes sense of the choice to embrace eternal hell.

Indeed, Lewis's sketch of the Big Ghost and his sense of entitlement and self- righteousness may help us to understand the rich man in Jesus' story. Perhaps both remain in hell because they are unwilling to embrace true repentance, holding instead to a perverse sense of self-satisfaction, though it comes at the considerable price of losing out on real happiness.

Moderating the Misery?

Before concluding, it is worth noting that Talbott has clarified his position in response to these criticisms. First, it is clear that at the end of the day, he believes that sinners who persist in rebellion against God and experience ever increasing misery as a result, finally have no choice but to turn to God. There is an upper limit to the amount of misery any finite creature can absorb, so the choice to turn to God if this point is reached is not free in the libertarian sense of the word. The choices we make to reach this point are free, but ironically, those choices take us to a point where our only option is to repent of all those choices.

Second, and more importantly, he has given us a clearer picture of what he means by the punishment that leads inevitably to repentance. Recall that I pointed out an ambiguity in his position insofar as he wants to affirm both "unbearable suffering" and "forcibly imposed punishment," while at the same time also repudiating the wrong kind of compulsion. He has now made it clear that he does not understand "unbearable suffering" and "forcibly imposed punishment in the same way they are typically understood in traditional accounts of hell, as some of his other writings suggested.

To illustrate the sort of suffering he has in mind, he offers the example of a foolish married man who has an affair with an unstable woman. Later, as an act of revenge she murders his wife and child. (He does not report the fate of the bunny rabbit). Talbott says the man's subsequent guilt, sorrow and sense of loss would be an unbearable suffering. God could use these to move him to repentance, and "insofar as God uses the man's suffering as a means of correction, or as a means of encouraging repentance, we can again say that the man has endured a *forcibly imposed punishment* for his sin."[31] Moreover, he points out "the good in the worst of sinners—the indestructible image of God if you will—can itself become a source of unbearable torment."

While these clarifications are very helpful for understanding Talbott's position, unfortunately, they are not so helpful for defending it. Indeed, these very clarifications produce a dilemma for Talbott that make his case for necessary universalism much less plausible. In short, it appears he must either give up his account of unbearable torment, or he must give up his claim that all sinners must reach a point where they can resist no farther. Talbott's claim that all sinners will reach a point where they cannot but give in to God is persuasive if God will indeed forcibly impose punishment that is literally unbearable. The problem, however, is that the way he has spelled out what he means by unbearable misery, it is not at all obvious that it must have this effect.

Let us come back to the example of the foolish philanderer. Granted that his actions and the subsequent course of events cause him great misery, is repentance inevitable? Surely God can use his suffering as a means of correction to *encourage* repentance, as Talbott notes, but there is nothing in the case as described that makes such a response inevitable. Rather than repent, he might become angry and embittered if he believes God allowed the murder of his wife and baby as a means of punishment for his affair. He might judge this a disproportionate punishment for his sin and come to see God as a vengeful deity who does not deserve worship and obedience. And as a result, he might move ever farther away from God in his rebellion, hardening his heart more by every step.

Consider this sort of case in view of Talbott's opinion that we have the freedom, "expressed in thousands of specific choices, to move incrementally either in the direction of repentance and reconciliation or in the direction of greater separation from God, and that freedom God always respects."[32] Now if this is true, it is far from clear why such incremental movement

31. Thomas Talbott, "Misery and Freedom: Reply to Walls," *Religious Studies* 40 (2004) 218.

32. Ibid., 221–22.

must inevitably shatter our illusions in such a way that we could not but repent and be reconciled to God. Indeed, it seems just the opposite would be the case. The more we move away from God, the more we harden our heart and dull our conscience, the more we rationalize our sinful actions, the less we will be inclined to repent and be reconciled to God. Objectively speaking, of course, such a person would be ever more miserable. But subjectively, the hardening and rationalizing make the misery more tolerable.

Of course, God could also cause increasing pain to us in other ways as we moved farther and farther away from him. He could, like a Spanish inquisitor, forcibly impose greater and greater physical pain upon us— tighten the screws so to speak with each such incremental move. And were he to do this, then surely we would reach a point where we would crack. But presumably Talbott would reject this as inappropriate compulsion, as I have argued above.

So again, Talbott has a dilemma on his hands, indeed a hell of a dilemma. He can either modify his account of divinely imposed unbearable misery or he can give up his claim that all sinners must eventually reach a point where they can resist God no farther. If the only forcibly imposed punishment God metes out is the sort described in his reply, there is no convincing reason why sinners could not continue to resist him forever. But if Talbott modifies his account of divinely imposed misery to make it truly unbearable, he will be endorsing the sort of compulsion he has repudiated as inappropriate. Moreover, he will undermine his claim that God allows us freedom to move ever farther away from him. I conclude then, that Talbott has not succeeded in making his case that the doctrine of eternal hell is incoherent and therefore not possibly true.

Conclusion

Hell still burns because it is an integral part of the web of beliefs that make up the orthodox Christian doctrine of salvation. Hell still burns because there is a broad consensus in the orthodox Christian theological tradition that scripture teaches eternal hell, at the very least that it is possible that some will be eternally lost. The burden of proof is on those who interpret scripture differently, and in my judgment, that burden has yet to be met. And hell still burns because human freedom makes it intelligible, if not likely, that some persons will choose their eternal misery rather than submit to the grace of transformation.

3

Purgatory in the Writings
of Augustine and Bede

Isabel Moreira

IN THE MODERN ERA, any historical discussion of Purgatory inevitably starts with the seminal study of Professor Jacques Le Goff, in which he posed the question: When was the "birth" of Purgatory?[1] This question, and even more his answer, has spurred debate for three decades and continues to draw scholars into the fray. While not minimizing the importance of earlier texts, including those that predated Christianity, Le Goff's quest was to find the origins of a purgatory that was familiar to the Catholic Church from the *end* of the Middle Ages. This perspective explains to a great degree the way he answered the question of origins, and why he focused on the twelfth century. Le Goff's definition of a fully evolved purgatory set a high store on a precise use of language: "Until the end of the twelfth century the

1. Jacques Le Goff, *The Birth of Purgatory* (Chicago: University of Chicago Press, 1984) translated by Arthur Goldhammer from the French, *La naissance du Purgatoire* (Paris: Editions Gallimard, 1981). See also Le Goff, "The Time of Purgatory (Third to Thirteenth Century)," in *The Medieval Imagination*, translated by Arthur Goldhammer (Chicago: University of Chicago Press, 1988; first published 1984) 67–77. Le Goff's contribution to medieval scholarship has been assessed in a collection of essays on his legacy, *The Work of Jacques Le Goff and the Challenges of Medieval History*, edited by Miri Rubin (Woodbridge, UK: Boydell, 1997).

noun *purgatorium* did not exist: *the* Purgatory had not yet been born."[2] Le Goff reasoned that the use of this terminology in the twelfth century allowed for a "spatialization" of thought that enabled medieval Christians to understand purgatory as a place that could be understood in architectural relationship to the more concretely understood places of heaven and hell. Thus Le Goff honed in on purgatory in its twelfth-century form because he believed he could show that it had become part of a clearly defined tripartite afterlife. This left any kind of purgatorial understanding prior to the twelfth century as an idea in embryo.

In the past three decades, much has changed in scholarship on purgatory. Some scholars have chosen to question—or at any rate refine—the frames of Le Goff's original claim. Some problems were quickly noted (*purgatorium* was used as a noun prior to the twelfth century, for example) but there was also a push to reappraise evidence for Christian belief in purgatory in earlier centuries.[3] But by what criteria can belief in a place of post mortem purgation be determined? Does it depend entirely on a consistently understood view of purgatory's architectural place in the afterlife? I have argued that it is significant to find the point at which the idea of post-mortem purgation was relieved of the heretical shadow of earlier patristic debates.[4] That led me to propose that purgatory was poised to enter the medieval Christian mainstream when the Northumbrian monk, Bede, presented purgatory to a Christian audience as a theologically accepted and acceptable belief. So in general terms, I place myself in the company of recent scholars who look to the story of purgatory's origins much earlier than the twelfth century.[5]

However, as scholars focus on the early Middle Ages, it is important to understand that the frame of inquiry has changed. For contemporary

2. Le Goff, *Birth*, 3.

3. It should be noted that Le Goff has held to the twelfth century as the century of purgatory's invention in more recent works; see Le Goff, *The Birth of Europe* (Oxford: Blackwell, 2005) 52.

4. I have proposed that an idea of purgatory can be sustained where there is evidence of functionality and theological viability, *Heaven's Purge: Purgatory in Late Antiquity* (Oxford: Oxford University Press, 2000).

5. Peter Brown, "The Decline of the Empire of God: Amnesty, Penance, and the Afterlife from Late Antiquity to the Middle Ages," in *Last Things: Death and the Apocalypse in the Middle Ages*, edited by Caroline Walker Bynum and Paul Freedman (Philadelphia: University of Pennsylvania Press, 2000) 41–59; Claude Carozzi, *Le voyage de l'âme dans l'au-delà d'après le littérature latine (Ve-XIIIe siècle)* (Palais Farnèse: École Français de Rome, 1994).

historians, the writings of the great figures of the Christian intellectual tradition must share space with other types of historical information such as visions of the afterlife, sermons, epitaphs, the liturgy, and florilegia. For this paper, however, I am going to focus primarily on the contribution of Augustine, but with a forward glance to Bede. Both figures have a place in the early history of purgatory but the respective weight given to them as "authors" of purgatory warrants scrutiny.[6]

As a way to illuminate the contrast between Augustine's time and Bede's, I think it is useful to present what we know about their preparations for death and the afterlife. Augustine's last days are described by his admirer and biographer, Bishop Possidius of Calama:

> [he] often told us in intimate conversation that the reception of baptism did not absolve Christians, and especially priests, however estimable, from the duty of doing fitting and adequate penance before departing from this life. And he acted on this himself in his last and fatal illness. For he ordered those psalms of David which are specially penitential to be copied out and, when he was very weak, used to lie in bed facing the wall where the sheets of paper were put up, gazing at them and reading them, and copiously and continuously weeping as he read.[7]

Furthermore, in the last ten days of his life, Augustine asked that no one disturb him except at the time when food was brought or the physician called, seeking to avoid outward distraction; "during the whole of that time he gave himself to prayer." This end was a meditated choice: Possidius informs us that Augustine was forcefully struck by accounts of

6. This is not the place to examine the works of Christian writers between Augustine and Bede. Gregory the Great's views on postmortem purgation, for example, are not examined here. The purpose of this essay is to highlight significant differences between Augustine and Bede.

7. Possidius of Calama, *Life of Augustine*, translated by F. R. Hoare (New York: Sheed and Ward, 1965) 31. Louis I. Hamilton situates this portrait of a weeping Augustine in the context of the imminent Vandal threat to the city, in "Possidius' Augustine and Post-Augustinian Africa," *Journal of Early Christian Studies* 12.1 (2004) 85–105. However, if we suppose the scene has some claim to authentic representation, Augustine's self-imposed seclusion in his last illness can also be seen on its own terms. Augustine's weeping is penitential and his seclusion reminds one of Plotinus's words on the purification of the soul: "The purification of the Soul is simply to allow it to be alone; it is pure when it keeps no company; when it looks to nothing without itself; when it entertains no alien thoughts. . . . Is it not true purification to turn away towards the exact contrary of earthly things?" Plotinus, *Enneads*, 3. 6. 5. translated by Stephen MacKenna (Harmondsworth: Penguin Classics, 1991) 193.

how other pious Christians had died.[8] Augustine must have been aware that his manner of death and preparation for the afterlife would be noted by his contemporaries.

Possidius goes on to inform his readers that: "after a service was offered to God for the peaceful repose of his body, he was buried." The last ten days of Augustine's life were spent in as much isolation as he could arrange, and he focused his remaining energies on penance. The penitential psalms that were his focus in his final days are recorded in later centuries as forming part of funeral activities. A simple mass preceded Augustine's burial.[9]

By contrast, Bede's last days present a rather busier picture.[10] Like Augustine, he knew he was dying. During the days that followed he continued to give lessons to his students as best he could, and spent his nights occupied in prayers of thanksgiving. He also hurried to complete, by dictation, two works on which he was engaged: a translation into English of the Gospel of John, and a book of excerpts from Isidore's *Book of Cycles*. Then, as death came closer, he distributed his few possessions to the priests of the monastery—pepper, handkerchiefs, and incense—asking each of them "to say masses and prayers for him with diligence." Bede's request for masses and his concern to distribute his few possessions to the priests who would perform that office, anchor him to an early medieval view of death that included a robust notion of purgatory and the actions needed to encourage a speedy release. His deathbed preparations are consistent with those of his peers.

In the light of these passages, it would be reasonable to suppose that the prospect of imminent arrival in purgatory and the need to mitigate its rigors was far more to the forefront of Bede's world than Augustine's. Augustine's austerity and isolation, and the simplicity of his burial, connects him closely with the funerary customs of the late Roman world. By contrast, Bede appears "medieval" as he drew people towards him for his final preparations.

8. Possidius, *Life of Augustine*, 27.

9. Very little is known about funerary activities in this era. For most Christians, the presence of clergy would not have been expected. For a recent discussion of the literature, see Éric Rebillard, "The Church, The Living and the Dead," in *A Companion to Late Antiquity*, edited by Philip Rousseau (Chichester: Wiley-Blackwell, 2012) 220–30. Damien Sicard's study remains the best source analysis of early funerary liturgies. *La liturgie de la mort dans l'église latine des origins à la réforme carolingienne* (Münster Westfalen: Aschendorff, 1978).

10. Cuthbert, *Letter on the Death of Bede (Epistola de obitu Bedae)*edited and translated by Bertram Colgrave and R. A. B. Mynors in *Bede's Ecclesiastical History of the English People* (Oxford: Clarendon Press, 1969) 579–87.

Yet it is Augustine, not Bede, who is most often identified with the theology of purgatory. It is still quite common to see Le Goff's appraisal repeated that Augustine was the "True Father of Purgatory."[11] This honorific suggests that we might expect to find the foundations of the medieval tradition of purgatory in Augustine's works. Indeed, Augustine is such a defining theologian for the Middle Ages that this is what we might expect. Augustine's works were broadly cited by medieval theologians, including on the topic of purgatory. Yet the reality of Augustine's contribution to the idea of purgatory is far from being so simple.

In what follows I will show that, far from being the "True Father of Purgatory," Augustine went to great lengths not to make a doctrinal stand on purgatory at all. This is not to diminish Augustine's contribution. Augustine *does* refer to an interim state for souls prior to the Last Judgment, and he *does* discuss at some length purifying fires at the Last Judgment, but he *does not* put these ideas together; there is no reference in *City of God* to purification by fire prior to the fire that immediately precedes the Last Judgment. Nor does he write about the purification of souls in the interim state by any other means. It is not possible to be exhaustive here, but in what follows I present a few passages commonly cited as evidence for Augustine's views on purgatory. The passages clarify two things: First, why progressive postmortem purgation was such a problematic notion for Augustine; and second, why purgatory could find no place in Augustine's interpretative schema for the book of Revelation as presented in *City of God*.

The strongest statements on postmortem eventualities are to be found in a little handbook—*enchiridion*—that Augustine prepared for a prominent layman, Lawrence, in response to his request for a reference work, a *vade mecum* on Christian teaching, that he could keep with him at all times. Its value is in its synthesis of Christian teaching, more than in theological exploration: Augustine hopes the book will nurture the already learned Laurence to become wise in the ways of God.[12] The work was written about

11. Le Goff, *Birth of Purgatory*, 61. Joseph Ntedika ascribed an "evolution of the doctrine of purgatory" in Augustine's thought in his 1966 study, *L'Évolution de la doctrine du purgatoire chez saint Augustine* (Paris: Études Augustiniennes). More recently, Heikki Kotila concedes that Augustine never defines the concept of purgatory, but asserts that in confronting Pelagian theology, "[he] gave more evidence of his belief in some kind of *post mortem* purification." *Memoria Mortuorum: Commemoration of the Departed in Augustine* (Rome: Institutum Patristicum Augustinianum, 1992). However, it is never indicated that this fire was anything other than the fire that all souls would go through on the day of the Last Judgment.

12. Augustine, *The Enchiridion on Faith, Hope and Charity*, translated by Bruce

AD 421 when Augustine was sixty-seven years old; he had been a bishop for twenty-six years. The brevity of the work complements its pastoral purpose.

"In the time intervening between a man's death and the final resurrection," writes Augustine to Lawrence, "the soul is held in a hidden retreat, enjoying rest or suffering hardship in accordance with what it merited during its life in the body." This idea—that the souls of the dead would experience rest or torment between death and the Last Judgment—was widespread in Christian thinking—Tertullian had imagined something similar at the beginning of the third century when he wrote that the souls of the faithful who were not yet in heaven would be in a place of refreshment, and certainly not in hell.[13] Indeed the passages are so close in sentiment and terminology, that it is possible that Augustine drew directly from Tertullian here. In this temporary abode, the soul experiences the state it will know at the Last Judgment. Neither Tertullian nor Augustine viewed the tormented souls in this interim abode as being purified. Rather, because Augustine perceived God's judgment as present and ongoing, directly after death the soul experiences joy or torment proleptically—in a kind of flash-forward to the fate that will be ultimately confirmed for it. This idea of anticipatory judgment would not have been viewed as diminishing the momentous nature of the Final Judgment when the dead would be raised, and all (except martyrs) would enter the fire and proceed to their final destination. As no-one deserves salvation, Augustine explains, it is Christ's action at the Last Judgment that will give "undeserved mercy" to the saved.[14]

Returning to the interim state, Augustine continues: "Nor should it be denied that the souls of the dead are eased by the piety of their living friends, when the sacrifice of the mediator is offered for them or alms are given in Church." However, in keeping with the pastoral nature of the work, Augustine cautions his friend Lawrence here: the souls for whom these services are profitable are those who "earned merit whereby such things could be of profit to them." But he goes on warn his reader: "let no-one hope to obtain any merit with God after he is dead that he has neglected to obtain here in this life."[15] Thus these prayers may only help those who have already acquired sufficient merit to make those prayers profitable. These prayers are

---

Harbert (New York: New City Press, 1999) prologue.

13. Tertullian, *De anima*, edited by Jan Hendrik Waszink, Corpus Christianorum 2 (Amsterdam: J. M. Meulenhoff, 1947) 55–58.

14. Augustine, *Enchiridion*, 24 [94].

15. Ibid., 29 [110].

a "solace," and "alleviation," or "consolation" to them, perhaps a psychological comfort that they have not been forgotten—but there is no indication here that such prayers alter their fate or shorten their time in that place. These souls must still wait for the Last Judgment, and at that point both groups of souls, the saved and the damned, will go through the fire.

Traditionally, an important feature of the fire at the Last Judgment is the notion that it will test the souls of those who enter it. Augustine's thought was that the fire did not judge souls, but rather that the fire exposed and cleansed the souls of the elect. It is therefore interesting to note how Augustine handles 1 Cor 3:11–15 where a powerful image and metaphor was used to describe the quality of the Christian life. The Christian, we read, builds on the foundation of Christ with gold, silver, precious gems, wood, hay and straw. When the Christian comes to the testing fire, those who have built with wood, hay, and straw (all combustibles) will "suffer loss though he himself will be saved, but only as through fire." In *The Enchiridion*, and elsewhere, Augustine explains that this fire is to be understood as a metaphor. For example, the "fire" can refer to tribulations in the present life, examples of which are loss, bereavement and even the pain of death itself. About five years after *The Enchiridion*, Augustine commented again on this passage in *The City of God*, where he proposed that the Christian who suffers loss is like the Christian who is too attached to a spouse.[16] Being married is not a sin, but earthly attachment exposes the Christian to the pain of loss—that is why some will experience pain in the afterlife as a kind of "fire." (Again—it is a metaphor). As in *The Enchiridion*, Augustine suggests in *The City of God* that the 'fire' may refer to any kind of tribulation, but now he goes further: tribulation may refer to the suffering at the end of the world, or it may refer to the fire at the Last Judgment. In short, Augustine suggests a number of ways to interpret this passage but he avoids endorsing any single view in favor of another. However, even in this exploratory frame of mind in *The City of God*, Augustine's suggestions reference only the final fire. Returning to *The Enchiridion*, Augustine does briefly consider the fire of Corinthians in terms of the afterlife. Again his language is very cautious: "*Nor is it beyond belief* that something of the same kind could happen also after this life and it can be asked if it is the case, whether or not an answer can be found that some of the faithful are saved by a kind of purifying fire more or less quickly, depending on whether they have loved perishable

16. Augustine, *City of God*, 21.26.

good things more or less . . ."[17] Again, by reference to the direction of Augustine's thinking in *The City of God*, the purifying fire envisaged here, that can clean off the dross of earthly attachment is most likely envisaged as the fire at the Last Judgment.

In fact, it is important to note how consistently Augustine discussed the fire of purification in the sole context of the Last Judgment. The refiner's fire in *The Prophecy of Malachi* is identified by him as having twin effects: it will purify the righteous in this life so that so that they will be entirely without sin; it will purify the Church as a whole at the Last Judgment by sweeping the damned out of the community.[18]

Furthermore, Augustine wanted to leave room for God to exercise his autonomy, even at the Last Judgment for he writes: "However, not all men who endure temporal pains after death come into those eternal punishments, which are to come after that judgment. Some, in fact, will receive forgiveness in the world to come for what is not forgiven in this, as I have said above, so that they may not be punished with the eternal chastisement of the world to come." That is to say, God can always intervene because God is God. This is the "amnesty" for sinners that Peter Brown connected so effectively with the Roman law and imperial practice.[19]

The entire notion of post mortem purgation was fraught with problems for Augustine and his contemporaries. Recent history had made the danger clear. Augustine was living in an intellectual environment where every strand that connected ideas and practices to an idea of purgatory was rife with difficulties—and those difficulties were represented by various groups of people who argued for one, or a combination, of all these ideas. Most notably, some Platonists promoted an active agenda of ritual purification, although this was only one end of the Platonist spectrum. There was also the Christian intellectual, Origen, who imagined the material cosmos as a divine purification machine designed for the sole purpose of redeeming

---

17. Augustine, *Enchiridion*, 18 [69].

18. Augustine, *City of God,* 20.25. "From these words it seems quite evident that in the judgment the punishments of some are to be purificatory . . . they are cleansed of their stains and purified in a certain sense when the wicked are separated from them by the penal judgment, and when the segregation and condemnation of the wicked effects the purgation of the rest, because thereafter they are going to live free from any contamination by such people."

19. Peter Brown, "Vers la naissance du Purgatoire: Amnistie et pénitence dans le christianisme occidentale de l'Antiquité tardive au Haut Moyen Âge," *Annales E.S.C.* 52.6 (1997) 1247–61.

souls and having no existence beyond that task. I call this the "no soul left behind" view. Augustine appears to have been reticent about engaging too deeply with Origen's thought. Platonists of various stripes were evidently fairer game, and in *The City of God* Augustine singled out Platonists for this error. There he states, "Now the Platonists . . . hold that all punishments are directed towards purification . . . whether suffered in this life or the next."[20] Somewhat unfairly, Augustine conflates Platonists of all sorts when he associates them with a reliance on purification rituals in this regard. But it is in his discourse against the Platonists that Augustine most clearly advances a theological reason why rituals of purification are not needed: Christ *is* the purifying "principle," he states, and by his incarnation he purified both flesh and spirit.[21] Thus there is no place for additional rituals of purification because Christians are "purified and healed" already, by Christ. This may have been an argument lobbed at Platonists but it signaled his way of thinking about Christian purification.

Finally, if we look at Augustine's interpretation of the book of Revelation in *The City of God*, we can see why purgatory had no logical space in this schema. Augustine upheld the message of the apocalyptic text by spiritualizing its message. Rather than limiting the significance of Revelation to a catalogue of future events as millenarians had done, Augustine embarked on an interpretation by which all that appeared to be a future action could be interpreted as present reality.[22] For example, the "heavenly Jerusalem" that will descend to the earth is not a future eventuality but a present reality: "This City has been coming down from heaven from its beginning."[23] The "kingdom of believers" has already arrived; the "last age" is already upon the world. Death (the first death) is when sin enters the soul; Resurrection (the first resurrection) is when Christ enters the soul. There will be a "last" judgment, but God's judgment is not confined to the last days: "God is even now judging, and he has been judging from the beginning of the human race."[24] There really is no place for post mortem purgation in

20. Augustine, *City of God*, 21.13; Plotinus, *Enneads*. 3.2.41.

21. Augustine, *City of God*, 10.24.

22. Augustine, *City of God*, Book 20 explicates this interpretation. On the background and implications of this interpretation with respect to millenarian thought, see Paula Fredriksen, "Tyconius and Augustine on the Apocalypse," in *The Apocalypse in the Middle Ages*, edited by Richard K. Emmerson and Bernard McGinn (Ithaca, NY: Cornell University Press, 1992) 20–37.

23. Augustine, *City of God*, 20.17.

24. Augustine, *City of God*, 20.1.

such an interpretive schema. Rather, Christ is the purifying, healing agent experienced in this world. No soul that has not already accepted Christ can expect to be purified by Christ in the next.

But as hard as it is to find evidence of purgatory in Augustine's thought, it must conversely be acknowledged that it can be equally hard to prove that it is not. Augustine did not state clearly—as he could easily have done—that there was no purgatorial activity prior to the fire of the Last Judgment. It has been suggested that the perfectionist theology of Pelagius which prompted Augustine's concern for the fate of the "mediocre" favored a stronger understanding of post mortem purification. In fact, this is not easy to show. As much as any other factor, this strategy of avoidance on Augustine's part points to his profound discomfort with the subject on many levels. His reticence is also a measure of Augustine's care to understand his sources and to think through all sides of an issue.

I think we have to keep this in mind as—it turns out—Augustine represents something of a hiccup in the developing notional arc of a Christian purgatory. It is pretty clear that many of Augustine's contemporaries thought that the pain of the soul's experience in the world must be connected in some way to its experience of pain in the afterlife, and ultimately to its fate. It was probably what most people dedicated to philosophy and religion believed: It was how they made sense of the presence of evil in the world and how they set a value on human suffering. This economy of suffering encompassed the realms of the living and the dead, and such notions informed future Christian cultures of belief in death and the afterlife. But Augustine was very resistant to the notion that any kind of "automatic system." He resisted any idea about salvation that limited God's agency and autonomy. He resisted the idea that the human could *do* anything to advance his or her own salvation in the afterlife, or alter God's judgment (whether mercy or condemnatory) through rituals. And this is why, in the end, Augustine could not commit to the idea of a progressive purgatorial place or time in the afterlife. He, perhaps more than most, would have been horrified to have learned that he had been termed "True Father of Purgatory."

From the bustling Hippo Regius of Augustine's day we now turn to the starkly beautiful Northumbrian coastal landscape of beaches, fields and rivers. Here stood small stone churches with small glass windows, and monastic houses furnished with niches and alcoves fit for a very few possessions.[25] Bede (673–735) a Northumbrian monk, was raised in a

25. Some seventh-century stone churches and minsters have survived in parts, or as

monastery from the time he was a little boy (he was an oblate—offered to the community by his parents).[26] There his life was ordered by the beauty of the Benedictine Rule. Bede comes across as an optimist who saw in the tranquil order of Christian life as he experienced it in the monastery, a pathway to union with God. A decade before his birth the great controversy over the date of Easter had been resolved at the Synod of Whitby (664) and with it an increasingly strengthened sense that Northumbria was part of the greater Christian community and that it had a special historical connection to Rome. Yet times had not always been peaceful. In Bede's youth Britain had been devastated by bubonic plague. It was said that Bede was himself one of the sole survivors when the plague hit his monastery. Yet as he describes it, Bede's time was an era of positive energy, when peace and tranquility allowed Northumbrian nobles and ordinary Christians to lay aside their weapons and take monastic vows.[27] The sheer sense of "belonging" to the Christian community was a powerful notion for Bede, and as he looked back at those earlier decades, an appreciation of God's present grace must have loomed large.

Bede's reputation among historians runs high—being a historian himself.[28] His reputation as a theologian has not always been so high, although that is beginning to change. Bede has the reputation of being an elegant consumer of earlier patristic thought, but not an original thinker. Yet Bede was not slavish in his use of patristic tradition, nor did he recoil from asserting patterns of Christian life that were familiar to him and that appeared pious and sanctioned by Scripture.[29] This is demonstrated in his engagement with

---

foundations for later building, but virtually nothing remains of wooden churches. Even simple edifices would have been decorated with painting and textiles, although they did not compare in size or technique with churches southern continental churches of the previous century. On Anglo-Saxon monastic sites, including some photos and plans of early sites, see Sarah Foot, *Monastic Life in Anglo-Saxon England c. 600–900* (Cambridge: Cambridge University Press, 2006).

26. George Hardin Brown, *A Companion to Bede*, Anglo-Saxon Studies 12 (Woodbridge, UK: Boydell, 2009) provides a helpful introduction to Bede's writings.

27. Bede, *Ecclesiastical History*, 5.23

28. Bede's reputation as a careful scholar has not diminished even as his aims and agenda have been better understood. See Alan Thacker, "Bede and History," in *The Cambridge Companion to Bede*, edited by Scott DeGregorio (Cambridge: Cambridge University Press, 2010) 170–89.

29. On the new appreciation for Bede's exegetical corpus and its wider availability to modern readers, see the collection of essays in *Innovation and Tradition in the Writings of the Venerable Bede*, edited by Scott DeGregorio (Morgantown, WV: West Virginia

Augustine and Origen, although it was an unequal level of familiarity. Bede knew a great deal of Augustine's views through his works; he undoubtedly knew much less about Origen.

So why is Bede important? Bede's writings do a number of things that are important to the formation of purgatory: They furnish a description of souls experiencing purgatory in a defined place in the afterlife in *The Vision of Drythelm*[30]; they outline an understanding of purgatory centered on the relationship between the living and the dead, and connect its operation and functioning with prayers for the dead, the masses, and almsgiving; and they grapple with Origen's views in order to open up a space for an orthodox delineation of a Christian purgatory.

There is no space here to rehearse the minute details of Bede's contribution to the history of purgatory—that argument can be found elsewhere. But it is fair to say that Bede was not beset by the doubts that Augustine's writings exhibit. Bede's preaching, like Augustine's, fully emphasize that those saved from eternal punishment were a special, chosen group—God's elect—but recognized that they might require lengthy purification in the fires of purgatory, and this would occur before Judgment Day. "They are either made clean from the stains of their vices in their long ordeal until Judgment Day, or, on the other hand, if they are absolved from their penalties by the petitions, almsgiving, fasting, weeping, and oblation of the saving sacrificial offering by their faithful friends, they may come earlier to the rest of the blessed."[31] Even in the worst case scenario, when confession was made only at the point of death, God's elect could hope to make full restitution in purgatory. Prayers, alms, and masses could actually bring about an earlier deliverance. The echo of Augustine's *The Enchiridion* here is instructive because where Augustine had stated that departed souls would feel some consolation or relief, Bede asserts that prayers can do something very specific—they can absolve sins so that the soul in purgatory can come earlier to a place of rest. There is no hedging here. Bede undoubtedly had *The Enchiridion* before him when he wrote this, but he understood Augustine through the lens of contemporary practices and beliefs that were by his time more clearly consolidated.

University Press, 2006).

30. *The Vision of Drythelm* is related in Bede, *Ecclesiastical History*, 5.12.

31. Bede, *Homily for Advent* in *Bede the Venerable: Homilies on the Gospels, Book One, Advent to Lent,* translated by Lawrence T. Martin and David Hurst (Kalamazoo, MI: Cistercian, 1991) 17.

Finally, Bede was not beset by vocal pagan opponents like the Platonists, nor was he cautious in his condemnation of Origen. He did not see Origen's universalism as a present threat. Origen had "abused God's grace" but for Bede, living in a Christian environment, purgatory did not threaten God's grace because it purified only the elect and he viewed it as compatible with an eternal hell. Bede directed his gaze at Origen and said, essentially: You are wrong . . . nevertheless . . . there is a purgatory.[32]

Returning to what we are informed about Augustine's last days, and Bede's last days, we can see that these vignettes illuminate the very different way these two Christian intellectuals were represented in their thinking about their needs after death. Augustine knew very well that his circle of friends would treat his body with respect and provide him with the funeral rites that, he had once written, would provide nothing more than a consolation for the living. Augustine's efforts were focused on purifying his mind, body and soul before death—eliminating other people from his chambers, and focusing on God in prayer. Bede also prayed in his little monastic cell with his body propped up so that he could face the little altar. But Bede also busied himself with the final preparations that would help him in purgatory. In recognition of the burden that such pious rituals entailed, he handed out his few possessions to those around him as gifts in pious reciprocity. At Bede's deathbed we can see that purgatory had found its place in the minds of the dying, and of those who tended them, as they prepared for what lay ahead.

32. For this "nevertheless" moment in Bede's *Commentary on Proverbs*, 2, xi, 7, see *Heaven's Purge*, 163: "Nevertheless, it should be noted (*notandum autem*) that if the wicked will not be saved, still there are those" (*sunt tamen qui*) who die with slight sins attached who can be absolved after death." Latin edition by David Hurst, *In proverbia Salomonis libri iii*, in *Bedae Venerabilis opera, pars ii: Opera exegetica*, Corpus Christianorum, series Latina, 119B (Turnhout: Brepols, 1983) 70.

4

The Pains of Hell and the Surprises of Purgatory:

Walker Percy's *Love in the Ruins*

Ralph Wood

ARTISTIC EXCELLENCE CONSISTS LARGELY in creating secondary worlds, reshaping the primary world in order to discern and to discover the deepest things of God's good creation. As Tolkien says, everyone is an artist, even if unawares. We are all makers, all poets. We are always and already fabricating both internal and external things. The products of our hands and our lives thus constitute greater or lesser works of art. Supremely imaginative artists working in a Christian mode invite their readers to enter the realms of hellish pain and purgatorial cleansing and paradisal joy. In every case, they engage our imaginations, taking us more profoundly into truth than perhaps either history of philosophy, though they too employ the image-making faculty.

History threatens to drown us in endless data, said Aristotle, while philosophy may hoist us into airy abstractions. Hence his acclamation of imaginative literature as offering a middle way that provokes thought by embodying it the concrete particulars of plot and character, of scene and voice and atmosphere. No wonder that C. S. Lewis declared that, while reason is the organ of truth, imagination is the faculty of reality. It gives ideas embodiment in irreducible form. There is no abstracting the essence of an at work into its bare kernel after shedding its husk. The two are inseparably dependent on each other. Art of this transcendent kind promotes either sympathy or horror by having us inhabit imaginary places and spaces, and in so doing it makes possible the radical renovation of our lives. In his essay on Dante, therefore, T. S. Eliot contends that we need not literalize the pilgrim's journey as occurring only in the afterlife and thus as having little immediate relevance. Dante depicts Hell, Purgatory, and Paradise so as to turn them, says Eliot, into present-day experiences and contemporary states of mind. So does the fiction of Walker Percy, I will argue, especially his novel titled *Love in the Ruins*.

I. The Pains of Hell

Walker Percy was born in Birmingham, Alabama in 1916, the son of a prominent lawyer who could trace his ancestry back to the Percys of Northumberland and an equally illustrious mother (Martha Susan Phinizy) who had French Catholic ancestors. At age sixteen, Percy was orphaned, together with two brothers, when his father committed suicide, using the same 20-gauged gun with which his own father had shot himself. As if the loss of his father were not enough to set Percy's life ajar, his mother died soon thereafter in a mysterious car-drowning. The three boys were adopted and raised in Greenville, Mississippi by William Alexander Percy, a distant kinsman. He was a distinguished planter-lawyer-poet as well as an ex-Catholic who had lost his faith and become a self-described Stoic. This noble man was to have a deeply shaping influence on Walker Percy, providing him a sterling example of the highly moral and cultured humanist who lives without recourse to Christian faith. Will Percy's memoir titled *Lanterns on the Levee* (1941) is an essential book for understanding Walker Percy's own life and work. In his preface to it, Walker says that he owes Uncle Will, as he called him, an unpayable debt.

Percy studied first at the University of North Carolina in Chapel Hill, where he won his BA degree in chemistry with high distinction. He then took his MD degree from Columbia University, concentrating in pathology, although he seriously considered psychiatry as his specialty. Yet Percy also spent three of his Columbia years undergoing psychoanalysis, a sign that he was a troubled man who would not be satisfied with the worldly success that he was already winning. During his residency in pathology at Physicians and Surgeons Hospital in New York City, as he was doing research on the cadavers of tuberculosis victims, Percy himself contracted the disease. He spent his long recuperation in an upstate New York sanatorium reading mainly philosophy and fiction, especially the work of Søren Kierkegaard and Albert Camus, Fyodor Dostoevsky and Leo Tolstoy, Jean-Paul Sartre and Thomas Mann—but also, thanks to a Catholic fellow-patient, the theology of Thomas Aquinas. These thinkers and artists probed the human condition, Percy discovered, in ways that made him wonder whether he was meant to be a writer rather than a physician.

Percy would never in fact practice medicine at all, though he would retain the diagnostician's impulse "to thump the patient and to find out what's wrong," as he said. Having gradually recovered from tuberculosis, Percy remained personally at sea, not knowing what to do with himself. He was a wanderer, both spiritually and geographically. He finally found clarity for his life when, in 1947, he married a nurse named Mary Bernice ("Bunt") Townsend and when, not long afterwards, they were both received into the Roman Catholic Church as converts. Percy would later confess that he owed his conversion largely to Kierkegaard's brilliant diagnosis of the modern malaise, but that he could not be satisfied with a fideist and individualist existentialism as the answer to it, and that he thus sought out the sacramental and prophetic faith of Rome.

The Percys eventually settled in Covington, Louisiana, across Lake Pontchartrain from New Orleans. Percy spent the remainder of his life there working as an essayist and novelist. He died in 1990 and is buried in the cemetery of a nearby Benedictine abbey beneath a gravestone identical to those of the monks, except that it is inscribed, quite simply, "Walker Percy May 28, 1916—May 10, 1990." During these forty-three years, Percy wrote six novels: *The Moviegoer* (1962); *The Last Gentlemen* (1966); *Love in the Ruins* (1971); *Lancelot* (1977); *The Second Coming* (1980); and *The Thanatos Syndrome* (1987). During these years he also penned two collections of essays, *The Message in the Bottle* (1975) and *Lost in the Cosmos* (1983). Other essays, reviews, and interviews were posthumously published in 1991 as *Signposts in a Strange Land*.

II.

Love in the Ruins is Percy's funniest novel. It is a mock epic, an antiheroic work. As such, it does not extol the highest virtues of American culture, as in traditional epics; instead, it exposes the worst stupidities in these latter days of our personal and cultural self-abandonment. Published in 1971, this futuristic dystopia is set in the Orwellian year of 1984, amidst a political crisis that threatens nuclear war. Its narrator-protagonist is Dr. Tom More, a physician living and working in New Orleans. Though More has been named in honor of Sir/Saint Thomas More, the noble Catholic humanist and martyr of the sixteenth century, this latter-day More is neither honorable nor godly. On the contrary, he is a self-confessed "bad Catholic." He does not depict himself in winsome terms:

> I, for example, am a Roman Catholic, albeit a bad one. I believe in the Holy Catholic Apostolic and Roman Church, in God the Father, in the election of the Jews, in Jesus Christ His Son our Lord, who founded the Church on Peter his first vicar, which will last until the end of the world. Some years ago, however, I stopped eating Christ in Communion, stopped going to mass, and have since fallen into a disorderly life. I believe in God and the whole business but I love women best, music and science next, whiskey next, God fourth, and my fellowman hardly at all. Generally I do as I please. A man wrote John, who says he believes in God and does not keep his commandments is a liar. If John is right, then I am a liar. Nevertheless, I still believe.[1]

It should be obvious that Tom More is far from satisfied with his self-indulgent life. He has given himself over to an antic and despairing decadence because he has found the alternatives completely untenable. The heart of the novel lies, in fact, in his acute diagnoses of what passes as political and religious life in America. He discerns, for example, that for all of their mutual anathematizing, the extremists on the right and the left are unconscious mirror images of each other. The Roman Catholic Church, for example, has renamed itself the American Catholic Church. It has established its headquarters in Cicero, Illinois, and it has adopted the image of a suburban house surrounded by a white picket fence as its logo. It also celebrates Property Rights Sunday, and the American flag is raised when

---

1. Walker Percy, *Love in the Ruins: The Adventures of a Bad Catholic at a Time Near the End of the World* (New York: Farrar, Straus & Giroux, 1971) 6. Further references will be within the text.

the priest elevates the Host. Liberal Catholics fare no better. They are agitating for the right of divorced priests to *remarry*. Evangelical Protestants are even worse off. They have given themselves over almost entirely to entertainment. They have even developed golf courses that can be played at night, and their tournament slogan is "Jesus Christ, the Greatest Pro of Them All." Proctology has become the medical science of the future, as the way to the truth lies in our bowels rather than our hearts or stomachs. Constipation is thus the conservative complaint, since conservatives can't *let go* of anything. Liberals, by contrast, suffer from diarrhea, being unable to *hold on* to anything.

Some of the novel's most hilarious passages describe this twinning of liberals and conservatives, who of course regard themselves as dread enemies.

> Some Southern states have established diplomatic ties with Rhodesia. Minnesota and Oregon have their own consulates in Sweden.
>
> The old Republican Party has become the Knothead Party, so named during the last Republican convention [1964] in Montgomery. . . . [They have printed] a million more buttons reading "Knotheads for America," and banners proclaiming "No Man Can Be Too Knotheaded in the Service of His Country."
>
> The old Democrats gave way to the new Left Party. . . . LEFT usually it is, often LEFTPAPA, sometimes LEFTPAPASAN . . . hardly ever the original LEFTPAPASANE, which stood for what, according to the Right, the Left believed in: Liberty, Equality, Fraternity, The Pill, Atheism, Anti-Pollution, Sex, Abortion Now, Euthanasia.
>
> The center did not hold.
>
> However, the Gross National Product continues to rise.
>
> There are Left states and Knothead states, Left towns and Knothead towns but no center towns . . . Left networks and Knothead networks, Left movies and Knothead movies. The most popular Left films are dirty movies from Sweden [depicting fellatio being performed in mid-air by parachutists.] All-time Knothead favorites, on the other hand, include *The Sound of Music*, *Flubber*, and *Ice Capades 1981*, clean movies all.
>
> Both political parties have had their triumphs.
>
> The Lefts succeeded in having "In God We Trust" removed from pennies.
>
> The Knotheads enacted a law requiring compulsory prayers in the black public schools and made funds available for birth control in Africa, Asia, and Alabama. (17–19)

As a theologically astute psychiatrist, Tom More is convinced that our twin diseases are *angelism* and *bestialism*. Like angels, we attempt to invent ourselves out of whole cloth, floating transcendently in the realm of pure possibility, denying our created condition as *embodied* souls, "of the earth earthy," as the Psalmist says. We abstract ourselves from the traditions and convictions that root us in time and place, becoming virtual angels orbiting the earth. Or else like beasts, we seek to plunge beneath our condition as rational animals by sinking into total physicality, denying our created condition as *ensouled* bodies. We immerse ourselves in comforts and conveniences, in money and possessions, becoming little more than contented animals.[2] In neither case do we remember Pascal's splendid description of the human condition as *ne ange, ne bête*, neither angel nor beast. Hence Tom More's attempt to create an encephalographic machine called a *lapsometer*. He takes its name from the Latin *lapsus*, or fall; for it allegedly can detect the extent from which we have fallen away from our true condition as angel-beasts and/or beast-angels. By means of complex brain stimulations, this sophisticated machine promises both to diagnose and to heal the riven condition of the American soul.

More blames Descartes and his epigoni for our late-modern sickness unto death. Hence his desire to turn his lapsometer into "the first caliper of the soul and [thus to supply] the first hope of bridging the dread chasm of Western man ever since the famous philosopher Descartes ripped body loose from mind and turned the very soul into a ghost that haunts its own house" (191). From Occam and Scotus to Kant and Newton and Locke, we Westerners have treated the activities of the intellect as a discarnate operation. We have regarded it as faculty existing independently of the body, and thus as abstracted from history and tradition and location. This phantom-like "soul" finds its only life in either autonomous ethical acts or subjective religious experiences. The moralism of the left is echoed by the pietism of the right, and both of them are individualist to the core. Gradually More discovers that the split state of American moral and spiritual life cannot be knit back together by the workings of even the most sophisticated machine. It requires a far more radical remedy, as More finally learns.[3]

2. Percy derives these dialectical opposites from his careful reading of Kierkegaard's *Sickness Unto Death*. My unpublished essay on this matter—"Four Comic Cases of Kierkegaardian Despair in Walker Percy's *Love in the Ruins*"—can be found on my website: http://www.baylor.edu/ralph_wood

3. Though his lapsometer is credited by the gullible, especially by those in the medical professions, and though it is actually patented by a Mephistophelean character

In the meantime, More becomes ever more discouraged. Though his nation seems to be prospering despite its deadly divisions of right and left, More himself is miserable. The three women whom he has at his beck and call cannot bodily satisfy him, nor can he stop the ramblings of his mind by endlessly guzzling gin fizzes. He prospers only when he is mocking the twin idiocies of our culture, since he can find no vital alternative to them. Gradually Dr. More begins to discern that he is living in Hell. Though his suburb is called Paradise Estates, it is in fact a precinct of Perdition. Unlike nearly everyone else, More detects the poisonous odors pervading the moral atmosphere like gas from an extermination camp. Far from being a place whose inhabitants might glimpse the Beatific Vision, it is a realm of unacknowledged Perdition.

Nowhere do these invisible hellish forces exert themselves more dramatically than in a scene involving Father Rinaldo Smith, the pastor of a small remnant of faithful Roman Catholics. One Sunday as he stands to deliver the homily, Father Smith falls stone silent, unable to utter a word. After the parishioners rush him to the sacristy, they then have him committed to a local psychiatric hospital, assuming that he has suffered a nervous collapse. There he explains his aphasia as a speechlessness that has not been caused by brain malfunction. He declares, instead, that "they're jamming circuits." He refers not to electronic gremlins or glitches but rather to the "principalities and powers." "They've won and we've lost," Father Rinaldo continues. "Their tactic has prevailed," he elaborates. "Death is winning, life is losing . . ." In one of the novel's most haunting sentences, the modest little priest confesses that "I am surrounded by the corpses of souls. We live in a city of the dead" (184–85).[4]

---

named Art Immelman, it proves self-evidently to be a fraud, except by powers of auto-suggestion. Those who think it is healing them find not a true cure but an excuse for enacting the worst of all states: a bestialism that is also angelic.

4. George MacDonald notes that such living death is often marked by its frenetic activity : "It is not the banished demon alone that wanders seeking rest, but souls upon souls in ever growing numbers. The world and Hades swarm with them. They long after a repose that is not mere cessation of labour; [but] a positive, an active rest. . . . [They] rush at anything to do—not to keep from thinking, for [they have] hardly begun to think, but to escape that heavy sense of non-existence, that weary and restless want which is the only form life can take to the yet unliving." *George MacDonald: An Anthology*, edited by C. S. Lewis (London: Geoffrey Bles, 1955), pp. 123–24.

III.

This, I submit, is the breakthrough prophecy that Walker Percy delivered more than four decades ago: Hell is not only a post-earthly state. It is also this present evil age that we now inhabit. Though we may outwardly thrive, we inwardly rot. We possess animal bodies without human souls. As Athanasius of Alexandria warned, early in the fourth century, it is possible for human beings to abandon the divine image and likeness in which we are made. We can undo our very nature, perversely turning it inside out like a sock, regressing to an anthropoid state:

> So then, men having thus become brutalized, and demoniacal deceit thus clouding every place, and hiding the knowledge of the true God, what was God to do? To keep still silence at so great a thing, and suffer men to be led astray by demons and not to know God? And what was the use of man having been originally made in God's image? For it had been better for him to have been made simply like a brute animal, than, once made rational, for him to live the life of the brutes.[5]

Blaise Pascal agreed with Athanasius that God stanches the loss of his rational creatures by becoming human in Jesus of Nazareth. Perhaps because he lived fourteen centuries later, Pascal was a good deal less sanguine than Athanasius. He described humankind as the weakest of all creatures, a slender and fragile plant, yet also a reed capable of metaphysical thinking. The far more pessimistic and apocalyptic Walker Percy goes Pascal not one better but one worse: He described our species as a "walking genital." Human beings who return to Hobbes's brutish state of nature are no longer unthinking animals, Percy contends, but deliberate, self-conscious beasts. Our brutishness is unlike that of the other anthropoids. The other animals copulate only when in season. Alone among all the zoological creatures, the humane female, usually prompted by male desire, can remain in a constant state of estrus, capable of intercourse at any and all times. Percy does not hide what happens when a culture becomes obsessed with sex, drugs, and all the other sensate stimuli of our time. It becomes bestial. In two of his last novels, therefore, he gives hellish fictional life to a culture that has become ever more savage and subhuman.

5. St. Athanasius, *On the Incarnation of the Word.* http://www.newadvent.org/fathers/2802.htm

The central scene in *Lancelot* is taken straight from Dante's *Inferno*. In his final novel, *The Thanatos Syndrome*, Percy goes beyond even Shakespeare's dire description of our kind as the "poor, bare, forked animal," the creature whom one of his characters calls "the beast with two backs." A later and much angrier Dr. Thomas More, the narrator of *Thanatos*, describes our latter-day coupling animals as having only a single back, the second now rendered redundant. Flirtatious women no longer use the frontal approach to arouse sexual desire in men; instead, they present themselves from the rear, to be mounted like dogs. These bestial copulators dare not look into each other's eyes and faces, lest they espy the final fading vestiges of the divine image.

Yet there is another variety of hellish anti-humanity that outrages Percy even more than our regression to hyper bestiality. We are surrounded by the corpses of souls in high places no less than low. The worst crimes are not committed by sordid malefactors whom we read about in the police reports of our newspapers. In our culture the deadliest evils are almost all perpetrated by the well-heeled, by barbarians with clean fingernails, as C. S. Lewis called us. The city of the dead is inhabited by the trousered apes whom Lewis describes in his 1961 Preface to *The Screwtape Letters*:

> I live in the Managerial Age, in a world of "Admin." The greatest evil is not now done in those sordid "dens of crime" that Dickens loved to paint. It is not done even in concentration camps and labour camps. In those we see its final result. But it is conceived and ordered (moved, seconded, carried, and minuted) in clean, carpeted, warmed, and well-lighted offices, by quiet men with white collars and cut fingernails and smooth-shaven cheeks who do not need to raise their voice.[6]

It is not difficult to identify these "last men," as Nietzsche labeled our latter-day *Homo sapiens*. During the previous century, more people were killed by violent means than in all of the preceding human centuries combined, roughly 180 million, most of them slaughtered by their own governments. Lest we think that such an indictment doesn't apply to the land of the free and the home of the brave, consider these data: Almost fifty-six million babies have been aborted since 1973 in the United States alone. More black babies are killed during any three-day period than the entire number of blacks who were lynched during the era of slavery and segregation. Twenty percent of all American pregnancies are now aborted, more than

6. C. S. Lewis, *The Screwtape Letters* (New York: Simon and Schuster, 1996) 8.

fifty million per year worldwide—most of them being performed, at least outside the West, on female babies. These are all manifestations of what, in *Evangelium Vitae*, Pope John Paul II called our nihilistic "culture of death." "The twentieth century will have been an era of massive attacks on life," he wrote in his hallmark encyclical of 1995, "an endless series of wars and a continual taking of innocent human life."

The pope observed the huge irony that, in an Enlightenment era that boasts of its discovery of inviolable human rights, "the very right to life is being denied or trampled upon, especially at the more significant moments of existence: the moment of birth and the moment of death." Once a nihilistic hedonism and physicalism have triumphed, the Blessed John Paul declared, the human body itself will be defiled:

> Within this same cultural climate, the body is no longer perceived as proper personal reality, a sign and place of relations with others, with God and with the world. It is reduced to pure materiality: it is simply a complex of organs, functions and energies to be used according to the sole criteria of pleasure and efficiency. Consequently, sexuality too is depersonalized and exploited: from being the sign, place and language of love, that is, of the gift of self and [the] acceptance of another, in all the other's richness as a person, [the body] increasingly becomes the occasion and instrument for self-assertion and the selfish satisfaction of personal desires and instincts. (*Ev. Vit.* 1.23)

Five years earlier, in the year of his death, Walker Percy wrote a letter to our national "newspaper of record." That the *New York Times* refused to print Percy's letter makes it all the more worth our hearing:

> The most influential book published in German in the first quarter of [the twentieth] century was entitled *The Justification of the Destruction of Life Devoid of Value*. Its co-authors were the distinguished jurist Karl Binding and the prominent psychiatrist Alfred Hoche. Neither Binding nor Hoche had ever heard of Hitler or the Nazis. Nor, in all likelihood, did Hitler ever read the book. He didn't have to . . .
>
> I would not wish to be understood as implying that the respected American institutions I have named [the *New York Times*, the United States Supreme Court, the American Civil Liberties Union, the National Organization of Women] are similar or corresponding to pre-Nazi institutions.
>
> But I do suggest that once the line is crossed, once the principle gains acceptance—juridically, medically, socially—[that]

innocent human life can be destroyed for whatever reason, for the most admirable socioeconomic, medical, or social reasons—then it does not take a prophet to predict what will happen next, or if not next, then sooner or later. At any rate, a warning is in order. Depending on the disposition of the majority and the opinion polls—now in favor of allowing women to get rid of unborn and unwanted babies—it is not difficult to imagine an electorate or a court ten years, fifty years from now, who would favor getting rid of useless old people, retarded children, anti-social blacks, illegal Hispanics, gypsies, Jews . . .[7]

Percy discerned that the asphyxiating gas of our anti-human humanism was having an especially deadening effect on the elites who occupy the high places of American cultural power. Hence his prediction that our misanthropic anthropocentrism would end by slaying bodies no less than suffocating souls. To speak of abortion as a reproductive right of refusal and of euthanasia as a private choice to rid ourselves of unwanted life—as if such killings were the equivalent of shopping for clothes or selecting an automobile—is to turn the moral life into a consumer's existence. To sow the seeds of cynical contempt for noncombatants with our anonymous drone attacks, having earlier laid waste to the jungles of Vietnam with carpet bombings and Agent Orange, is to reap the whirlwind of mass murders, pandemic suicides, and the assorted other psychopathologies of our time. It is, in sum, to dwell in an earthly Hell.

IV.

The danger of my recourse to the fiction of Walker Percy in analyzing the hellish character of these latter days should be obvious. It is what our ancient foreparents called "the fascination of abomination." Unless we are exceedingly careful, we can fall secretly in love with the things we allegedly loathe. Even Friedrich Nietzsche discerned that if we stare long enough into the heart of darkness, it will stare back at us. For this reason, I suspect, Dante gives us the barest glimpse of the triple-headed Satan. For in horrible parody of the Holy Trinity, he masticates the world's three worst traitors to their own lords—Judas, Cassius, and Brutus—as he himself lies fixed in a frozen lake of ice. The heart of Dante's Hell is not characterized by its

7. Walker Percy, *Signposts in a Strange Land*, edited by Patrick Samway (New York: Farrar, Straus & Giroux, 1991) 350–51.

heat, lest it give off warmth and light. At the core of Perdition there is sheer frigidity and thus utter lifelessness.

We are not meant to go there, even by way of prolonged imaginative inspection. We are meant, instead, to remember Leopold von Ranke's reminder that "every age stands equidistant from God." Already in the New Testament, we learn that Satan is the Prince of this world, and thus that the first century was already regarded as "this present evil age." Our own time is distinct but not unique. Insofar as Hell remains a perduring phenomenon, it will take different form in different agers. Hence the fallacy of regarding our time as uniquely damned. Such false perception will lead us to assume that we therefore must separate the wheat from the tares, the heavenly from the hellish. The enduring Christian quality of J. R. R. Tolkien's *The Lord of the Rings* lies precisely in such a refusal: Gandalf and Frodo and their weak little Company of Nine Fellow Walkers refuse to become fixated on the Evil One whom they are called to overthrow. Though with enormous difficulty and at terrible cost, they refuse the most hellish of all temptations. Though they are not yet Christians, even at best proto-Christians, they refuse to do what our Lord expressly forbids—namely, to answer evil with evil: to employ the weapons of Sauron against Sauron. To kill the great Necromancer—the Sorcerer of Death—with the Ring of Absolute Power that he had once forged in the volcanic fires of Mt. Doom, the Ring that they have come providentially to possess, would be but to create a new Sauron. We might even call him a Christian Satan, as our Lord called his first Vicar when Peter commanded him to avoid going up to Jerusalem, to avoid Golgotha, perhaps to lead a Maccabean-like revolt against the tyrants of Rome.

So it is with us. Many Christians are convinced we must "take back America," on the assumption, of course, that it was a good thing that we Christians once were in control of this county. We must rescue our nation, so the argument goes, from its seemingly hellish descent. We must employ the same weapons of political power used by enemies of the Kingdom. Even more grandiosely, we must rouse ourselves to restore Western civilization from its imminent collapse. Against such appeals to *Realpolitik*, Chesterton reminded us, the Church has already survived the collapse of two civilizations—the Roman and the Medieval—and there is no reason to believe that the coming of the Kingdom will not prevail against the gates of our present Hell. Such impatience was one of Walker Percy's perennial temptations. He referred often Oswald Spengler's 1918 book on the sunset of Western culture, *Der Untergang des Abendlands,* "the going under of the evening land," as Walker Percy liked literally to translate it.

The summons for us Christians to unsheathe our swords in order to topple Hell has received an even more convincing reply from Pope Emeritus Benedict. Even when he was still Cardinal Ratzinger, he made the astonishing confession that we Christians are likely to remain a minority faith for the foreseeable future—barring, of course, a miraculous outpouring of the Holy Spirit on our contemporary Gehenna. We are back where we began, Benedict confessed. We are a minority faith in an overwhelmingly pagan world. Nor is this an unambiguously evil plight. On the contrary, the emeritus pope calls us to create enclaves of Christian excellence—i.e., small communities of radically confessing and radically practicing Christians. There we will need to form our own newly minted Christian culture, drawing upon our bi-millennial Tradition, of course, but also fashioning new and unabashedly Christian arts and sciences and perhaps even technologies:

> Perhaps the time has come to say farewell to the idea of tradition-ally Catholic cultures. Maybe we are facing a new and different kind of epoch in the Church's history, where Christianity will again be characterized more by the mustard seed, where it will exist in small, seemingly insignificant groups that nonetheless live in an intensive struggle against evil and [that] bring good into the world—that let God in.
>
> The church will, in the foreseeable future, no longer simply be the form of life for the whole society. . . . The church will be . . . more a minority Church; she will live in small, vital circles of really convinced believers who live their faith. But precisely in this way she will, biblically speaking, become the salt of the earth again. In this upheaval, constancy—keeping what is essential to man from being destroyed—is once again more important, and the powers of preservation that can sustain [man] in his humanity are even more necessary.[8]

I maintain that this call to a modest rather than triumphalist kind of Christianity can best be likened to what the Church has traditionally en-visioned as the purgatorial life. Before making this case, it is important to answer the hoary Protestant canard that Purgatory is a halfway station be-tween Heaven and Hell. Quite to the contrary, Purgatory is a virtual vestibule to Paradise. None who enters it ever relapses to the Inferno. Instead, all of

8. Benedict XVI, *The Salt of the Earth: The Church at the End of the Millennium.* An Interview with Peter Seewald (San Francisco: Ignatius, 1997) 16, 164.

its penitents ascend the seven-storey mountain in order finally to be transported into the endless ecstasy of the Beatific Vision. Yet first they must first undergo a voluntary rather than a coerced cleansing of the unshriven sins that had clung to their mortal lives. Though this purification is painful, they eagerly embrace it, daring not—indeed, wanting not—to face God with anything less than pure hearts and wills. Some of these pilgrims require longer and more arduous cleansing than others. Dante himself, for instance, must be unburdened of the three evils that beset him more than all the others: pride, anger, and lust. Echoing the sentiment we heard from T. S. Eliot at the beginning—namely, that a properly Dantesque understanding of the afterlife requires our present participation in these post-earthly states—Alisdair MacIntyre has rightly identified Dante's *Purgatorio* as the great moral book of the West, our main Christian manual for living the virtuous life.

Walker Percy regarded the hour as far too late to be concerned about Paradisal delights. At his worst, he employed his art to spew venom against the Culture of Death and the Age of Ashes. Angrily and often impatiently, he warned of the wrath to come, as if he were himself the bringer of this final sentence of Doom. He likened the aim of his work, in fact, to the function of the proverbial canary in the coal mine. When the oxygen supply falls low, the bird keels over and the miners make their hasty exit. So does Percy, when he operates as scold, bid us to abandon this earthly city to its own sorry devices. At his best, however, especially in his early work, he fictionally depicts a more excellent way. It is not a heavenly so much as a purgatorial pathway. For the same Thomas More whom we have seen dwelling in Hell begins to discover that the demons in his own life need to be driven out.

Four of these purgatorial moments stand out from others. Early in the novel, More bursts out in both rage and grief, as he slashes his wrists on Christmas Eve. He attempts this nihilist act of self-murder after watching Perry Como—presumably a Catholic of Italian descent—dressed nattily in his cardigan and sitting contently on his stool, as he croons sacrilegiously about the holiest night of the year: "I'm Dreaming of a White Christmas." Yet, like the prodigal son, the self-lacerating More suddenly "comes to himself," squeezes his bleeding wrists into his armpits, and hobbles like a hobo to the house of a doctor friend to be sutured. "Bad as things are still when all is said and done, one can sit on a doorstep in the winter and watch sparrows kick leaves" (97). Yet something far greater is required of More than such a quiet Panglossian resignation to his own little garden spot. Thus does he commit himself to the psychiatric ward at a local hospital.

There he enjoys some of the happiest moments of his life. Among the other demented souls, he's thoroughly at home. Percy thus suggests that, in an hour as late as ours, the only sanity may be found in a certain kind of insanity, as he recalls:

> Here I spent the best months of my life. . . . In the day room and in the ward we patients came to understand each other as only fellow prisoners and exiles can. Sane outside, I can't make head or tail of people. Mad inside, we signaled each other like auctioneers, a wink here, a wag of finger there. I listened and watched. Outside there is not time to listen. Sitting here in the day room the day after Christmas next to a mangy pine tree decorated with varicolored Kleenex (no glass!) . . . my hands on my knees and my wrists bandaged, I felt so bad that I groaned aloud an Old Testament lamentation AAAAIEOOOOOW! to which responded a great silent black man sitting next to me on the blocky couch: "Ain't it the truth though." (105)

Yet More cannot dwell permanently among the deranged. His dormant Catholic conscience reminds him that his troubles are far more self-generated than culturally induced. Hence this remarkable confession, even as he still flirts with the pretty nurse who attends him in the hospital and whom he will eventually marry:

> Later, lust gave way to sorrow and I prayed, arms stretched out like a Mexican, tears streaming down my face. Dear God, I can see it now, why can't I see it at other times, that it is you I love in the beauty of the world and in all the lovely girls and dear good friends, and it is pilgrims we are, wayfarers on a journey, and not pigs, nor angels. Why can I not be merry and loving like my ancestor, a gentle pure-hearted knight for our Lady and our blessed Lord and Savior? Pray for me, Sir Thomas More.
>
> Etcetera etcetera. A regular Walpurgis night of witches, devils, pitchforks, thorns in the flesh, upkneed girl-thighs. Followed by contrition and clear sight. Followed, of course, by old friend morning terror. (109)

Like his fictional creator, More will not let us sentimentalize this deeply Augustinian confession that evil is a terrible nothing, a privation or absence of good, and thus the pain of absolute loss. More knows that he must re-order his loves to the love of God, lest he continue to twist and pervert his joys into a deathly Hell of his own making. Yet he lacks the will to do it. As Augustine taught, his will is turned in upon itself—*incurvatus in se*—and thus requires transcendent deliverance. Hence the spiritual ennui of More's repeated "etceteras," his slothful indifference to the good that he knows would require him to leave off his whoring and drinking.

What is required of him is nothing less than a purgatorial and Eucharistic life. This becomes evident in More's hilarious exchange with his Jewish physician, a friend ironically named Gottlieb. Here Percy reveals both the existential hell of American hedonism as well as the true cure for it. Gottlieb regards "lovemaking [as] a natural activity, like eating and drinking," and so he cannot fathom More's calling it "sinful and guilt-laden" when practiced outside marriage (116). In a hilarious dialogue of the deaf, More tries to explain to the spiritually opaque psychiatrist why—without a penitential and Eucharistic life—he is truly a dead and damned soul:

> "What I don't see," [Gottlieb declares], is that if there is no guilt after *une affaire*, what is the problem?"
>
> "The problem is that if there is no guilt, contrition, and a purpose of amendment, the sin cannot be forgiven."
>
> "What does that mean, operationally speaking?"
>
> "It means that you don't have life in you."
>
> "Life?"
>
> "Yes" . . .
>
> "What does 'purpose of amendment' mean?" [the addled Gottlieb asks].
>
> "Promising to try not to do it again and meaning it." (117)

The penultimate revelation that marks the beginning of More's *vita nuova*, comes near the end of the novel, as he proves finally unable to resist the twitch upon the tangled thread of his life. It occurs when he ponders the refusal of his daughter Samantha to seek out a miraculous cure in the baths at Lourdes. In one of the novel's darkest confessions, More explains why he did not take her there himself:

> I don't know Samantha's reasons, but I was afraid that she might be cured. What then? Suppose you ask God for a miracle and God says yes, very well. How do you live the rest of your life?
>
> Samantha, forgive me. I am sorry you suffered and died, my heart broke, but there have been times when I was not above enjoying it.
>
> Is it possible to live without feasting on death? (374)

Here Percy strikes deep. More confesses that he is himself is the chief denizen of this latter-day hell. He has found a curious delectation in the wretched condition of his own culture, living a funny-sad life of satirical mockery. So long as the world lies in ruins, why shouldn't he remain content with his lusting and drinking? Our worst fear, Percy suggests, is not that God is dead but that he is all too much alive, nearer to us than our own breath, knowing us infinitely better than we know ourselves. It is indeed a fearful thing to fall into the hands of the living God. The Gospel of Jesus Christ demands nothing less than it gives—namely, everything. There are no half measures. Total transformation is the strict requirement of the purgatorial life that we are called to live in making our exit from this present hellish age.

And so, in a redemptively reverse manner, More finds himself backing into the Kingdom. When Rinaldo Smith, pastor of the little Catholic remnant, seeks to shrive him on a Christmas Eve five years after the novel's main action closes, More confesses his sins in a single sentence: "I do not recall the number of occasions, Father, but I accuse myself of drunkenness, lusts, envies, fornication, delight in the misfortune of others, and loving myself better than God and other men" (397). Though More can make his *confessio oris*, he is powerless to exhibit any *contritio cordis*. He has no sorrow of heart. He is what Graham Greene called a burnt-out case, a virtual corpse of a soul incapable of feeling much of anything, whether delight or regret. All he can say is that he is sorry for not being sorry. Father Smith knows that, in the marvelous economy of grace, a double negative constitutes a bare minimal positive. Accordingly, the humble priest assigns More an appropriate *satisfactio operis*: this bad Catholic physician must make public penance by dousing his hair with ashes and wearing a sweater made of burlap. And so More attends midnight Mass for the first time in many years, eating Christ once again and thus having life restored to him. Early on Christmas morning, therefore, More finds himself embarking on his stumbling path toward Paradise:

> Barbecuing in my sackcloth.
>
>   The turkey is smoking well. . . .
>
>   The night is clear and cold. There is no moon. The light of the transmitter lies hard by Jupiter, ruby and diamond in the plush velvet sky. Ellen [his wife] is in the kitchen fixing stuffing and sweet potatoes. Somewhere in the swamp a screech owl cries.
>
>   I'm dancing around to keep warm, hands in pockets. It is Christmas Day and the Lord is here, a holy night and surely that is all one needs.

On the other hand, I want a drink. Fetching the Early Times from a clump of palmetto, I take six drinks in six minutes. Now I am dancing and singing old Sinatra songs and the *Salve Regina*, cutting the fool like David before the ark or like Walter Huston doing a jig when he struck it rich in the Sierra Madre. (402)

Conclusion

Walker Percy gives fictional life to our contemporary Hell ruled by the Prince of this world in both its bestial and angelic expressions. He reveals that we are already inhabiting a City of the Dead consisting of the corpses of souls. Percy warns against slothfully resigning ourselves to existence in this earthly Hell, even though we know that it will eventually work its own self-destruction. For in the meantime, it horribly increases its population if we stand idly by, allowing it to suck unnumbered unique and irreplaceable persons into its terrible maw. Yet he also cautions against our rising up in wrath against these demonic forces of damnation, lest we remake ourselves in their image by returning evil for evil. Nor does the more excellent way lie in the redemption of solitary souls in some allegedly individualist Christianity. It is found instead in the corporate and communal life of the Church. There we are called to the purgatorial life of prophetic and sacramental existence, so that we might get a foretaste of the glory divine that awaits the redemption of our bodies as members of Christ's Body.

5

Beatitude: What Heaven Is Like[1]

Paul J. Griffiths

I'm GRATEFUL AND HONORED to be here. My thanks are due especially to Mike Root for the invitation, and to all of you for being here to listen and discuss. The Center for Catholic and Evangelical Theology does splendid and important work, and I'm always pleased to be connected with its events as I've had the good fortune to be on occasion in the past.

My topic is beatitude, or what it's like to be in heaven. There's a standard Christian story about what happens to human creatures like us when we die, almost every element of which is shared by Catholic, Protestant, and Orthodox Christians, as well, probably, by those Christians who would prefer to use none of these labels. It'll be useful to have the part of that story that ends with beatitude, which is the same as to say with heaven, in our

---

1. The text that follows is substantially that delivered on 11 June 2013 at a symposium on heaven, hell, and purgatory sponsored by the Center for Catholic & Evangelical Theology in Baltimore. I'm grateful for the discussion the piece received then, and for the many interesting points of criticism raised. That I've not engaged those criticisms doesn't mean I don't take them seriously; but it seemed better to print the piece as given rather than to expand it as substantially as would have been necessary to respond to those criticisms. A more detailed treatment of most of the points made telegraphically here may be found in my *Decreation: The Last Things of All Creatures* (Waco, TX: Baylor University, 2014).

minds before we go on to entertain together some more speculative questions about heaven, so here it is.

1. Getting to Heaven

The first moment in the story is the last in this life: it's the first death, the death of the body. This occurs at the moment when the soul, the *anima*, separates from the body, that delicate fleshly organism an instance of which stands before you speaking right now. When that happens, the creature that was a human person is, temporarily, no more; what remains are the traces or vestiges of that person.

Some among those vestiges are material: they are the person's fleshly remains, his or her *corpus*, or corpse. As soon as the soul separates from the body, the person's fleshly traces begin to disaggregate, whether by rotting or in some more violent way. Ordinarily, the corpse will have disaggregated within a few dozen years sufficiently that it is no longer recognizable to anyone living. The corpse, everyone would agree, is not a human person; it is, at most, a human person's material remains. It does not, however, exhaust the remains of the now-dead person.

There are also psychic traces, the ordinary name for which among Christians is the soul, now separated from the body which it had until the moment of death informed. This too, the separated soul, is not a human person, and that is because human persons are constitutively and definitionally ensouled bodies, or, if you prefer, embodied souls. Anything that lacks either body or soul is by definition not a human person, and is therefore not a person at all.

But this is not to say that the dead person's traces, whether physical or psychic, are nothing at all, or are without interest. This is evident by what, according to the Christian story, happens to them next. The separated souls are judged by the Lord immediately upon death, as soon as they separate from the body. I'll leave aside the criteria for this judgment, itself a complex topic, and say only that Christian orthodoxy requires the view that some (perhaps all, but certainly some) separated souls are judged worthy eventually to live in eternal and unsurpassable intimacy with the triune Lord who created them. This group, the souls bound for heaven, does not immediately enter it, however, and this for a variety of reasons which, again, it would divert us too far to go into now. Common to all the heaven-bound souls, whatever their differences, is that they will reach their final beatitude, their final degree of intimacy with the Lord beyond which there is nothing more exalted, nothing greater or newer, only when their bodies are resurrected so that their souls can be rejoined with them and they can thereby become once again the human persons they once were. Once this has happened, those judged worthy to do so enter heaven. Separated souls cannot do this even though they can enjoy to some degree the beatific vision, the delightful vision of the Lord. The full, unsurpassable, heavenly vision of the Lord is possible only for human (and angelic) persons, and since human persons do not exist without bodies, they enter heaven only when the general resurrection has occurred and they are once again enfleshed with the self-same flesh they once had.

Even the person's physical traces are not nothing. The dead body is ideally treated with reverence, and its place honored. Relics, which is another name for the physical traces of a person (body parts and other objects that were intimate with the person while he or she lived) are objects of importance in the Church's life, as well as in the lives of those who remember the dead. And, it is in some sense the very same body—*idem numero*, identical in number, the self-same, as the Latin scholastics like to say—that will be resurrected at the end, to join again with the soul and thus to reconstitute the person.

That's the story. It's an interesting and complex one. It rests upon a particular understanding of human persons as embodied souls, psychophysical unities. These come into being at conception, continue in being until the separation of soul from body that is their death, continue then for a while—perhaps a long while—only as physical and psychical traces, and are then reconstituted (resurrected) as a precondition for entering heaven.

The lineaments of this story, the story of souls bound for heaven, are firmly grounded in the tradition's authoritative sources, which is to say in Scripture, creeds, conciliar texts, and (for Catholics) other authoritative magisterial texts. But not much else about heaven is so grounded. If you think for a moment about the credal confessions of the Church, whether Apostles', Niceno-Constantinopolitan, or (even) Pseudo-Athanasian, you'll agree with me, I'm sure, that while they are at one in their promise of eternal life to the faithful, they are equally unanimous in having nothing much to say about what it is like, the means by which it is attained, or the process of getting there. Scripture says not much more, at least not explicitly, about these matters. And for Catholics, while there is a little more given dogmatically about the nature of heaven than is contained in the sketch

I've just given—for example, that it is indefectible (one you're there, you don't leave) and that it never comes to an end—it doesn't amount to all that much. Christianity is doctrinally parsimonious in matters of eschatological detail, and for good reasons: these are mysterious matters, about which it is reasonable to think that our capacities for understanding are bound to be very limited. This lack of doctrine, however, is matched by luxuriance in speculation at every level of the tradition—there are visions, theological speculations, novels, poetry, hymns, paintings, musical compositions, and much more, in which more or less detailed pictures of what heaven is like are given. But I will leave these aside, fascinating and important though they are. I want instead to think with you about what heaven is like, rather than to try to imagine it. Imagination is an over-rated faculty anyway, and thought an under-rated one, so let's try what we can do by thinking, within the generous constraints of orthodoxy, about heaven.

2. How to Think about What Heaven Is Like

Restricting our attention to heaven as it is for human creatures (though they are certainly not the only creatures present there) we can say that heaven is our glory, the last thing for which we were intended and for which we hope. A glorious last thing for any creature, we can say with formal confidence, necessarily involves the preservation of all goods proper to the creature in question, as well as the maximization of those goods capable of a maximum. That's the positive rule. The negative form of the same rule is that a glorious last thing involves the removal from those creatures that enter it of any and all damage they have suffered between conception and the first death. With the preservation and maximization of all the goods proper to a creaturely kind, together with (what is really another way of describing the same state of affairs) the removal of all loss and lack and damage from it, the creatures belonging to that kind have reached their glory. They are in heaven, existing now in heavenly mode.

This is a useful but very abstract pattern of thought. It permits easy and accurate definition of what it is for a creature to be in heaven, and it moves thought about the matter in a certain direction. In order to put flesh on its bones, decisions need to be made about which are the goods proper to human creatures, and, concomitantly, about what counts as damage to them. Some such decisions are easy enough, or seem to be; and some of them are even given dogmatically for Catholic Christians, such as the

view that flesh is a good proper to human creatures, which at once entails
the conclusion that heavenly human creatures are fleshly, as we've already
noted. The separation of soul from body that occurs at death is an instance
of damage that heaven will heal. But many are not so easy. Consider the
property, *having active relations to nonhuman fleshly animate creatures*. If
this is a good proper to human creatureliness, then this fact may entail the
continuation of such relations in heaven by means of the presence of such
creatures there. But it is by no means obvious that this is a good proper
to human creatures, which is why Christians who have thought about it
have arrived at no consensus on that question. There are similar difficulties
about what counts as damage to human creatures. The pattern of thought
in play here, then, fundamental and essential though it is, is limited in its
yield, and seeing the nature of these limitations clearly should moderate the
degree of confidence we have in the judgments we make about such matters. Nevertheless, the yield of this pattern of thought is far from negligible.

We Christians have some further aids to judgment about which are
the goods proper to human creatures.

One among these is that we have a form of life given to us that we
know to be supremely good for us here below, and know therefore also to
foreshadow more fully than can any other form of life what life in heaven
will be like. The form of life I have in mind is liturgical. This is our foretaste
of heaven, and attending to its structure, purpose, meaning, and effects
upon those who engage in it tells us something about what heaven is like,
and about what it will seem like to human creatures to be there, to arrive
at a glorious last thing. Thinking about the liturgy, then, is helpful for ar-
riving at conclusions about what are the goods proper to human creatures.
Thinking in this way, however, also does not yield easy conclusions. We
must, for example, try to discriminate what is proper to the liturgy from
what is accidental to it; we must also make some ticklish decisions about
what it is that the liturgical life does to those who live it. It is easy to be
wrong, substantively or by way of emphasis, about matters such as this.
Nevertheless, attending to the liturgy is the closest we can get, here below,
to attending to heaven.

Attending to Jesus and Mary is another aid to reflection upon the
question of which are the goods proper to human creatures, and, therefore,
upon the question of what heaven will be like for us. If, as Christian doctrine requires, the resurrection and ascension of Jesus show us something
of heaven, and if, as doctrine also requires, heaven is the place where the

ascended flesh of Jesus and the assumed flesh of Mary are to be found, then thinking about that flesh—the flesh of each of those people—must have something to tell us about what heaven is like and about what it is like for human creatures to be there. Again, it is not at once obvious what we learn about heaven by attending to the risen Jesus and the assumed Mary; but attending to them is necessary if thought about the last things is to yield what it might.

3. Experience in Heaven

Suppose we understand "experience" very generally to mean "what it seems like to you to be you." Much of the time, when you're in dreamless sleep say, or for some other reason, it doesn't seem like anything at all to you to be you. But often it does. There's often a flood of sensory and affective and (even) intellectual seemings: you feel hot or cold or hungry or worried or bored or in pain or pleased at having solved a mathematical equation or ecstatic in the arms of your lover, or . . . well, you can fill in a lot more blanks. We are, that is to say, at least some of the time, conscious beings, and we share this with many, perhaps most, other living beings. They too feel hot, cold, hungry, and so on, even if in particular ways that we cannot easily imagine because of the deep differences between our bodily nature and theirs. Consider, for instance, what it seems like to a bat to locate itself in three-dimensional space by echo-sounding. You'll discover that you can't.

But the kinds of experience I've just mentioned—first-order seemings, we might call them—aren't the only kinds of experience we have. We also layer or stratify our experience, and one of the ways in which we do this is to take them to be ours, as belonging to us. This possessive layering is most clearly evident in states such as boredom, embarrassment, delight in praise, and response to threat. Consider, for instance, what happens when you overhear a conversation about yourself. What you overhear might be an anatomy of your defects or an encomium to your virtues. In either case, there'll be ordinary auditory experience: you'll hear some things. But you'll also categorize what you hear as about you, not about someone else, and it will therefore become quite different for you than would a conversation about someone you don't know casually overheard on the subway or the bus. The affective feel of your response to this possessively-layered experience will ordinarily be intense, and it may include smug self-satisfaction, anger, embarrassment, revulsion, and more. A useful shorthand for possessively-layered experience is "the inner theater." It's on that stage, surrounded with eye-lined mirrors, that you play out the drama of what it seems like to you to be you—and that's a pretty important drama for most of us here below, I should think.

Now let's think about this in terms of the principles of eschatological thinking we've already laid out. Is possessively layered experience, the inner theater, a good proper to human creatures, or is it an instance of damage? If the former, it will be present in heaven; if the latter it will not. I want to suggest to you that possessively layered experience is an instance of damage, an artifact of the fall we might say, and that it will therefore not be present in heaven.

Here are some reasons for thinking so:

The first is that the inner theater is unnecessary for most human activity, and indeed very often absent. Habit is its enemy, and when I am engaged in an activity that I've done often before, it often doesn't at all seem to me that I am doing it. Rather, it occurs. Consider, for example, the ordinary gestures of etiquette—the handshake, the bow, the ritual greeting. I don't have to decide to perform these; all that's necessary is the appropriate situation. When I'm introduced to you and I shake your hand, the inner theater's stage is just about empty. As we shake hands or air-kiss or whatever it is that we do, nothing about the texture of our experience—its phenomenology, if you want the twenty-dollar word—requires us to layer what we're doing possessively, to note it as ours. Indeed, were we to do that, we precisely wouldn't be being polite, but rather something much worse, something that might require judgments about our respective worthiness to have this etiquette-exchange. It's exactly the gift of etiquette that it doesn't require decisions like that. We can, I suggest, do most of what it's important for us to do here below without the inner theater.

Here's a second brief example of habit as experience's enemy, this one perhaps a little more controversial. I mean the activity of writing. I do a good deal of this, and, so far as I can tell, I ordinarily do it largely without any sense as I write that it is me writing, that this writing is mine; neither, ordinarily, do I note and categorize the first-order seemings that do occur to me—the feel of fingers on keyboard, for instance, or the changing visual patterns as words take form on the screen in front of me. The experience that does occur, first-order and unlayered, passes mostly at a low level of intensity, demanding and receiving little attention. Some of it can be reconstructed retrospectively without too much difficulty: I can recall, later, that the telephone rang while I was writing, or that no antonym for "categorical" came rapidly to my fingers. But at the time of writing, all that can, and usually does, remain below the conscious level—and it certainly requires no possessive layering, no inner theater.

This may seem odd. Doesn't writing involve searching for the appropriate word or phrase, imagining the balanced syntax of a well-ordered sentence in advance of tapping that sentence out on the keyboard, actively considering various lexical alternatives, and so on? In some sense it must involve all these, and more; but in terms of what seems to me to be going on, experientially, there is nothing like this. The sentences are formed in very much the same way as the gestures of etiquette are performed; and the processes that permit their formation are about as evident to me as I write as are the causally connected chains of physical events that make it possible for me to shake the hand of someone I meet—which is to say, not at all. As I write, the words flow; sometimes there is accompanying first-order experience, but more often not; and, after a while, something has been written. An advantage of this way of thinking about what it seems like to writers to write is that it moderates our tendency to think of what we have written as ours, which is, theologically speaking, pure gain.

One of the rules of thought I suggested earlier, in thinking about the heavenly life, was to attend to the liturgy as the clearest foretaste of heaven we have here below. How does this help us with the question about the inner theater?

Living the liturgical life requires, like any other complex communal practice extended over time, the establishment of habits of body and speech on the part of its practitioners. It is much less clear that it requires the establishment of habits of layered, possessive experience. Developing the required habits of body and speech may require that explicit instruction be given by those who are already practitioners to those who would like to be. The church has recognized this, and provides it by catechizing adults preparing to undertake the liturgical life by way of baptism's ritual death and rebirth. But even when such instruction is given, it plays an insignificant part in becoming a habituated liturgical agent—someone who knows how to live the liturgical life, how to go on, what to do next. Vastly more important is simply living it, doing what those who are already living that life do. As we become habituated liturgical agents, our sense that it is us—me, this particular person—worshipping the Lord is increasingly attenuated.

But it's not just that liturgy habituates. Baseball and piano-playing do that, too. Liturgy habituates in a particular way. There's a lot to say about this, and I've time to make only one among the points I'd like to make—and I should say that it's now, more than at any other point in this talk, that it'll be evident that I'm speaking as a Catholic. You may have to do some translation.

Liturgical agents, those who have become habituated to the worshiping work of the Christian people, have learned to act as do those who accept a gift of love. They have, that is, learned what it means to respond gratefully to a loving gift given freely outside the economy of exchange: a gift given without establishment of obligation, without expectation of return, and without calculation about the merits of the recipient. There is reasonable debate about whether gifts of that sort are possible. Ordinarily, perhaps always for us, gifts are given within the economy of exchange: the transfer of a good from one person to another carries obligation with it and, when it is accepted, establishes a bond of reciprocal intimacy between giver and recipient that permits return of the gift. But the liturgical life is a performance rich with signs that what is being celebrated in it is exactly the pure gift, the gift that establishes no debt and expects no return. The Lord owes us nothing; and to that we might add that he demands nothing from us. He simply, preveniently, and endlessly, gives. The liturgical life is in very large part a training in how to receive such a gift as that.

For example, as you enter the church building, you bless yourself with holy water from the baptismal font and genuflect before the sacrament reserved in the sanctuary's tabernacle. As the drama of the Mass unfolds, you will, seriatim, stand to listen to the Gospel proclaimed; sit to receive its exposition; stand again to begin participation in the sacrifice performed upon the altar; kneel after the Sanctus as the elements are consecrated; stand again to recite the prayer given by Jesus; kneel to confess your unworthiness to receive Jesus into your house, in imitation of the centurion appealing to Jesus to heal his sick servant; and then receive the body of Christ on your tongue.

This constant up-and-down writes upon the bodies of those who perform it frequently a habit of acting as an unworthy recipient of a prevenient gift. This is not to say that those whose bodies have been so written upon will, as a result, be able to provide an account of how their bodies have been overwritten, or of what that overwriting may be taken to mean. Doing that will be as common among liturgical agents as is giving an account of their language's grammar and syntax among those who speak it well—which is to say vanishingly rare. But whether or not the skill of theoretical articulation is present, permitting your body to be overwritten by the Lord's sentence of eternal life as given in the formalized play of the liturgy alters you as agent exactly in the direction of attenuating the inner theater.

The proper end of the liturgical life, I suggest, is the radical attenuation of experience. The inner theater is at best epiphenomenal to the liturgical life, which is also the Christian life, and at worst inimical to it. What that life points us to, and what it provides a real participation in, is a condition in which the one thing we will then do, which is to praise the Lord who gives, has no significant place for experience. The end of possessively-layered experience, for those resurrected for salvation, is its erasure. It will not seem like anything to the saints in heaven to be who they are. They will not identify the flood of seemings that is their heavenly life as belonging to them, being their own. Their existence will, grammatically, be entirely dative—they will be constantly addressed by the Lord's voice, and constantly confronted by his face; and their response will be exclusively one of adoration, to which the inner theater does not and cannot belong. They will have become habituated to the repetitive stasis of the praise-filled gift-exchange in such a way and to such an extent that the self-reflexive understanding of themselves as such is impossible, and would be a trivial distraction if it were possible.

4. Heavenly Flesh

We humans are fleshly creatures. That is given dogmatically and scripturally, and is part of the grammar of Christian orthodoxy. Attending to the end of Jesus' earthly life, which was by way of the ascension of his resurrected flesh into heaven, and to the end of his mother's earthly life, which was by way of the assumption of her flesh into heaven, only underscores all this. Flesh is a good for humans, and, thus, it will be present, perfected, in heaven. Until it is, we will not be fully there.

What can we say more than this? What is heavenly flesh like? We need to begin by saying something about the flesh here below, which is what we know.

Locatedness is intrinsic to the flesh in all its states. Being enfleshed locates us by giving us a place in the world, whether it's this devastated world, the edenic one, or heaven itself. To be flesh is to be here, somewhere particular, not everywhere, and not somewhere else. This is not to say that fleshly creatures are located, or find themselves in a place, as inanimate creatures do. For those latter, locatedness is exclusively spatial, and a complete account can be given of it by specifying Cartesian coordinates of space. The GPS software on your smartphone tells you all you need to know, for instance, about the place of the building we're in now. But your locatedness, as flesh, means something more than this. It means, also, an erotic relation, one of desire or delight or their opposites, to the place you're in. The spatial location of mere inanimate bodies is evenly distributed, mappable geometrically by coordinates and representable with mathematical precision on a grid. But the being-in-place of flesh is always uneven, stumbling, incapable of adequate representation on a grid. For flesh, there is holy ground and unhallowable, the soft and welcoming place and the place of despair; and the distance between such places is not capable of measure by rule. When the flesh is located by GPS at a place in the world, and represented by a glowing blue dot on the Google-mapped screen of your smartphone, it is being shown as a body; showing it—locating it—as flesh rather than as body is beyond the skill of software. For that, you'd need a device that could show space gathered and furled and concentrated and distended, a panorama of shrines and altars and places of pilgrimage as well as of death pits and bomb sites and concentration camps. Flesh genuflects here, is embraced there, is fed elsewhere, and flees in horror through devastated places elsewhere again. The map of its locatedness would be more like a weather map of isobars unevenly concentrated into zones of high pressure and low than like a gridded plain on which all places are alike. Inanimate body is undifferentiatedly present in all the furled and folded spaces of the flesh— the glowing Google-mapped dot of location is the same for all inanimate bodies even though the flesh knows the difference.

The extent to which you are fleshly rather than bodily is the extent to which place is given you under the sign of desire and delight. Flesh in heaven has its locatedness in constant awareness of its place before the risen flesh of Jesus and the assumed flesh of Mary. Fleshly locatedness in heaven is, then, a matter of repetitively static ecstasy, in the strict, etymological sense of that word—heavenly flesh stands outside itself, worshipping and being loved.

As well as being located, flesh is fundamentally and essentially erotic, desirous and delighting, or repelled and disgusted, that is, in all its states and conditions. The flesh's erotic character is not, as we perhaps most often and easily think of it, a drive or appetite internal to itself by means of which it relates itself to a world external to itself. On that model, the flesh's eros is what moves it toward the world, what motivates it to ingest, touch, and enter into the world. A lover, on that understanding, begins as a self-enclosed monad, and seeks contact with other such monads: she is a lonely aspirant to love until she finds other flesh with which to connect. But this way of thinking has it backwards. The flesh's eros is received as gift, not possessed as aspiration: it's only by being caressed, for example, that fleshly persons are capable of caressing; it's not that we are brought into being as caressers, awaiting occasion for the exercise of that potency. No, in order to be lovers, those capable of caressing (rather than merely touching) the flesh of another, we need first to receive the other's caress. That is, the lover becomes such only by receiving the gift of herself or himself as beloved. The flesh's eros, on this more adequate view, is received as gift, and necessarily so.

This is an implicitly theological view of the flesh's eros, of course, and I'll return in a moment to an explicitly theological construal of it. But it is also a view that coheres well with what we know of the growth and change of human persons as infants. Babies receive the gift of their flesh as erotic, as desirous of and erotically responsive to the flesh of others, only by being caressed, usually, at least in the first instance, by their mothers. Absent the maternal caress, the eros of the baby's flesh remains surd, unvoiced, and inactive, a possibility unrealized. Babies and small children—and indeed the young of other mammals—systematically deprived of the fleshly caress fail not only to be eroticized themselves, but also to flourish in other ways. Death, in fact, is the ordinary outcome of such deprivation. It is also the case that newborns do not have a good sense of the boundary between their own flesh and both the inanimate world of objects that surrounds them and the flesh of others. You can see this in a baby's surprise when it gums or sucks its toes with sufficient energy that it feels the result. The sense that the flesh has boundaries, and that the erotic is the principal mode of the flesh's interaction with what is outside itself, is learned, and is learned by receiving the caress, whether of inanimate objects or the flesh of others. Eros, then, is received as gift, and once received is intensified, shaped, and ornamented, by repetition.

Consider, in this connection and for example, the kiss. Becoming one who kisses is dependent, causally (and indeed definitionally) on being kissed. The impress of the lover's lips on one's own provides the gift of being one who, in virtue of being kissed, can kiss. Kissing is not a possibility for the unkissed; the flesh's eros, concentrated in this case in the lips, is without

remainder received from without. Furthermore, the extent to which the
flesh's eros appears to function non-reciprocally, not in response to gift but
rather by autonomous self-generation, is the extent to which it is a simu-
lacrum of eros rather than the real thing. This account can be extended
without much difficulty to all the other aspects and dimensions of the flesh's
eros, though I won't do that here. The key point to bear in mind is that the
flesh's trembles of desire before the flesh of others are possible for it only
if and as it is first desired. To say, "I love you," then, is to return a benison
received, not to make an offer. It is, ideally, something said simultaneously,
lip to lip and eye to eye, in harmonious counterpoint, not a tentative word-
bridge thrown across the gulf between one person and another. On this
model, unrequited love is something close to an oxymoron, and when it
appears to occur, that appearance is always evidence of erotic damage or
confusion of one kind or another.

The theological version of the flesh's receipt of itself as erotically
charged is not far to seek. Its charter text is 1 Cor 4:7, where Paul asks what
he has that he has not received. He expects the answer "nothing." The gift in
this case is the Lord's to us; the kiss, too, is the Lord's, as the opening verse
of the Song of Songs says: "Let me be kissed with your mouth's kiss," we read
there. And if you accept that the addressee of these words is the Lord, and
the petitioner a representative of us all, then what is being asked for here
is the gift of the flesh as erotically capable because itself loved and desired.
This is the erotic version of the doctrine of creation out of nothing. Our
flesh—we as fleshly—are not properly thought of as autonomously or by
nature possessed of the capacity to desire, a capacity which can seem then
be actualized by receiving the gift of being desired. No. Our very fleshliness,
eroticized, is brought into being *ex nihilo* by the Lord's kiss. The only thing
we can do about it is to open our mouths to the kiss, or to turn our faces
away from it. And in heaven's ecstatic locatedness we endlessly, repetitively,
open our mouths for that kiss and thus return it.

Should we be resurrected for eternal life, that fleshly condition will be
maximally social, maximally erotic, located in a flexed and furled space-
time in which every moment of desire is also one of delight, and in which
we are in fleshly relation to all the saints and, especially, erotically and de-
lightedly, with the risen flesh of Jesus and the assumed flesh of Mary. A
consummation devoutly to be wish'd.

5. Heaven's Population, Heaven's Lineaments

I've suggested, speculatively of course, that when you're in heaven it won't seem to you like anything to be you, even though you will be maximally happy, blissfully in beatitude. The bliss of beatitude, I think, requires exactly this conclusion; another way to put this is to say that an essential part of what beatitude consists in is erasure of the damage to our sense of ourselves produced by the fall. In the fall we became self-conscious self-possessors; in heaven's beatitude we shall leave all that behind, and will delight in the fleshly and intellectual vision of the Lord which is what we were made for, and all this in deep, non-possessive fleshly intimacy with the other saints in heaven that our resurrected flesh makes possible. There's much more to say about what heaven is like, and I'll end this talk by indicating what the main topics are, and, in utterly summary fashion, what should be said about them.

First about heaven's population: What's there? Angels, certainly: all the unfallen ones; we will join with them in the endless liturgy of praise. Humans, certainly: we know some of their names already—they are the saints—and we hope for our own presence there and for the presence of all those human creatures who have ever lived or ever will live. Other animate creatures, probably: it belongs to the human good to have relations with nonhuman animate embodied creatures, and that is, if not reason enough, at least good reason for thinking that there will be such creatures in heaven, and that we will be related to them as we should be. And inanimate creatures as well, probably: the heavens and the earth will be renewed, and if it is proper to human fleshly locatedness to have a place among other bodily creatures, inanimate as well as animate, then they will be there too.

And last, about heaven's lineaments. Heaven must be a place of a sort, a locus in which there is flesh. That much we know. And if, as the speculative parts of the tradition are close to unanimous in affirming, space and time are inseparable one from another and constitute the fabric of the created order's relation to the Lord who is not himself spatio-temporal, and have, along with all the rest of the created order, been damaged by the fall, then the renovation of the heavens and the earth will involve the renovation of space-time. That is a large and difficult topic; all I'll say about it now is that the metronomically measurable fabric of space-time to which we're accustomed here below will, in heaven, have become what it always was, which is folded around and enfolded by Jesus Christ, who is its center and heart and meaning. If you'd like to help me move talk like that out of a figurative key and into a formal-abstract one, perhaps we can do that in discussion. For now, for the time being, that's enough: heaven, perhaps, can wait, but the end of this talk cannot. I thank you for your time and attention, and I look forward to discussion.

6

Preaching Heaven and Hell

Victor Lee Austin

THERE ARE, I SUPPOSE, people in every congregation who wish their pastors preached more about hell. Generally speaking, these are not the people we want to encourage, at least in this attitude. God has always had followers who are keen on having the riot act read to other people; it is the role assumed in the Gospels often by the Pharisees. And indeed it may be said that the only people to whom Jesus read the riot act were the people who wanted him to read the riot act to others.[1] So we who preach naturally feel a reluctance to take up the topic of hell, lest we contribute to that unwarranted sense of self-righteousness. Rather than fall into the trap of T. S. Eliot's Becket, who sees the greater treason is "to do the right deed for the wrong reason," we preachers avoid doing the right deed in order to avoid acting from the wrong reason.[2]

I say that preaching on hell is an instance of "doing the right deed" because I assume that hell is an aspect of revealed truth and that to preach the fullness of revelation is the call of the preacher. Of course, one might decide that hell is in no way part of the Christian revelation—and if one

---

1. I owe this formulation to Andrew Mead.

2 T. S. Eliot, *Murder in the Cathedral*, 3rd edition (London: Faber and Faber, 1937) 44. Becket calls it "the greatest treason," since in the play it is the last of four temptations.

came to that conclusion, one in fact should not preach on hell. For the rest of this essay, however, I assume there is something to be said about hell, and that preachers should attempt to say it, despite the difficulty of doing so without encouraging self-righteousness.

Heaven, too, calls for homiletic attention, and it has its own peculiar difficulties. The common cultural assumptions about heaven are often at odds with Scripture and church teaching. In the Episcopal Church, the proper title of our funeral service is "The Burial of the Dead." But it is hard to exaggerate the cultural resistance to using that title for that service. Much more common is something like "A Celebration of the Life of Joe Schmo." I once teased our Fifth Avenue, New York City congregation about this in a Sunday sermon, saying that in such a service, in which we remember and honor and celebrate the life of a person we never quite admit has died, we recall so many good things about that person that we come to the end with the thought, that although this is our loss, it is God's gain.

So there are difficulties of preaching hell and preaching heaven. In what follows, I look at three occasions where preaching can touch on these matters. First there are the liturgies of the Triduum, especially Good Friday but also Maundy Thursday and the Great Vigil of Easter. The second is a funeral service—any burial service or memorial or requiem that follows upon the death of a member of the Christian congregation. And the third is any of the Sunday liturgies when the people have assembled and the Scriptures touch on death or eternal judgment or life after death or resurrection. To keep this manageable, I will treat these three occasions with examples and admonitions, and not try to be complete and comprehensive. Were I a German, this paper might be called "Notes toward Preaching Heaven and Hell."

At the liturgies of the Triduum, sermons are necessary. Although Christian liturgy conducted with fidelity and dignity conveys its own meaning and should not be reduced to pedestrian explanation, still it is necessary to make concrete proclamation in the particular preacher's living voice. Such sermons must be short: five to seven minutes is best, in my humble opinion, because there is so much else in the liturgy. And since short, they cannot exposit every detail of the liturgy, or indeed every detail of the rich scriptural narratives of the day. A stringent selectivity is essential.

To shape one's sermon toward the question of heaven and hell, one might notice that the Triduum has an overall shape of humiliation, of descent down and down (cf. Phil. 2:5–8). One might consider that the Triduum shows us that, to be a real inhabitant of heaven, one must be able to come down and down some more. And by implied contrast, the real inhabitant of hell has no freedom of humility.

So one might preach on Maundy Thursday about the footwashing alone: the refreshing kindness of cool water bathed upon tired feet, and how, to give us this kindness, getting down there at the level of our feet, Jesus performs a sort of pageant of the Incarnation. One might then conclude with a look to the morrow. At the supper, Jesus takes off his garment in order to wash the feet. At the cross, Jesus sheds everything in order to save his disciples.[3]

On Good Friday, one could begin at death. I did so once, in this manner: "At the end of the day what we have is a corpse. His muscles no longer move; his brain cells issue no commands; there is not the slightest movement in his chest; the blood no longer circulates; his flesh is cold as stone, and there it is, lying in chill darkness, closed over and put away."[4]

So far, this could be the death of anyone. But then we may give voice to our particular loss: "At the end of the day we begin to realize that we will never again hear his voice. He will not tell us another of his stories. We won't walk alongside him on the road; we won't find him across from us at table. And we know that we are only just beginning to feel the enormity of our loss."

Again, this evokes the universality of our experience of death. It sinks in, maybe when you go to bed that first night after your wife has died, that you will never again hear her voice. And we also know everything isn't all right. That's true generally, but particularly so on this night of the holy week: "At the end of the day we have terrible memories. There is guilt. He had so much to tell us, and we were asleep. He had shared his soul with us, but when it got dangerous, we ran away. And there is nightmare: the

3 Raymond Brown takes the footwashing to be "a prophetic action symbolizing Jesus' death in humiliation for the salvation of others." He also notes that the verb in John 13:4, *tithenai*, "laid [down]" (here, Jesus' garment) is the same as used in John 10:11ff. for laying down one's life. There is a further parallel in that the same verb is used for taking up his garment and for taking up his life. Raymond E. Brown, *The Gospel According to John (XIII–XXI)* Anchor Bible (Garden City, NY: Doubleday, 1970) 562, 551.

4 Direct quotations in this section are from the author's sermon on Good Friday 2006 at Saint Thomas Church Fifth Avenue.

brutality of what was done to him! The shame of his nakedness; the whip, the thorns in his scalp; the sneers. Nails through nerves; dehydration; suffocation. These images in our memory of torture and abandonment: how will we ever get over them?"

And I concluded: "At least the pain is over now. Yet it's *all* over, isn't it. All that's left of his voice, his vitality, his dream—all that's left, at the end of the day, is this corpse."

Except, of course, that's not how it turned out to be. What is particular about the passion in John's Gospel, read on Good Friday, is its emphasis on Jesus' kingship, how he is control throughout everything that happens. Now you could say that pedantically, or you could try to evoke it. Here's what I ventured: "As the stun of it settles in, the mind goes back and starts to tarry over some small bits of remembrance, things not noticed earlier. . . . Did you see how he was calm through it all? He knows he will be betrayed; calmly he states this truth at supper. He goes to the garden; there his betrayer comes with an arresting party. He addresses them with authority . . . and it is not he but those who would seize him who fall to the ground." And with some other details, we can recollect Jesus' strength through it all, how he created new family from the cross, and so forth. "Even though they were killing him, he was choosing to allow himself to die." And: "When they nailed him to the cross, they put him upon his throne. There . . . he became king, drawing to himself all who hear his voice." So yes, "we have a corpse. But not only a corpse. Today a kingdom has been brought into being." That kingdom, I did not need to say, was the kingdom of heaven.

So during the Triduum, one may speak of the downward movement that is, surprisingly, the triumph of God and the inauguration of the heavenly kingdom. But the time is limited, and I do not think one can preach much detail about heaven and hell then.

At a funeral a similar stringent focus is needed—in this case, because of the emotions of the bereaved. Sermons at funerals must be short also. Nonetheless, at a funeral it is especially necessary for truth and mercy to kiss each other (cf. Ps 85:10).

First, with regard to speaking the truth: one must avoid canonizing the departed. We do not want to suggest that God is getting a pretty good person here and he better be properly appreciative. For at the time of death, most particularly, human beings are confronted with the mystery that our existence itself is and has been God's gift. Herbert McCabe quotes Wittgenstein: "Not *how* the world is, but *that* it is, is the mystery."[5] The first mystery is not how we have lived (perhaps better, perhaps worse) but that we have lived at all. So when life ceases, when the last breath is drawn and then there is stillness, we must not pretend that we understand. Creatures cannot get their arms around the Creator; comprehension—literally, getting our prehensiles all around what we would make into our object—is impossible.

The Order for the Burial of the Dead in the Book of Common Prayer exercises epistemic humility in many ways.[6] It is explicit in one of the intercessions, new to the 1979 Book: "Help us, we pray, in the midst of things we do not understand, to believe and trust in the communion of saints, the forgiveness of sins, and the resurrection to life everlasting."[7] Death is something we do not understand—indeed, I would assert, cannot understand.

Another area of epistemic humility concerns the state of existence of the person who has died. Please do not imply in the sermon that she is looking down on the ceremony and making comments. And do not suggest that her spirit is floating around and, for instance, continues to live in our hearts. We don't know any of those things. And there is no hint of them in the burial office.

In particular, we should not say that the departed has gone to heaven. The burial office speaks of "heavenly" (an adjective) much more often than it speaks of "heaven." Heaven, the noun, occurs precisely three times: in the Lord's Prayer, and in one other prayer (a voice from heaven proclaimed, blessed are the dead who die in the Lord),[8] and in an optional anthem new to the 1979 Book: "Christ will open the kingdom of heaven to all who believe in his Name . . ."[9] Yet even in that last case it is "the kingdom of heaven" that is opened to believers, and not "heaven" plain and

5. Herbert McCabe, *God Matters* (London: Geoffrey Chapman, 1987) 5.

6. I quote from the Book of Common Prayer 1979 of the Protestant Episcopal Church in the United States of America, commonly called the Episcopal Church. All official editions have the same pagination. In quotations from this Book, I have changed the italicized pronouns, which refer to the deceased, from masculine singular to feminine singular. In this section of the paper, my comparisons of various Prayer Books has been immensely aided by Paul V. Marshall, *Prayer Book Parallels*, vol. 1 (New York: Church Hymnal Corporation, 1989).

7. Page 481, an optional intercession.

8. This is an optional additional prayer, new to the 1928 Book and repeated in 1979.

9. Page 483.

simple. Nowhere does the burial office speak of entering heaven. We have then an epistemic reluctance, at the least, to name "heaven" as the postmortem destination of the faithful. Of that which we do not know, the liturgy does not speak.

Faith, however, being an epistemic virtue, does know things, and here we can speak truth that is also merciful. Faith knows, to be most basic, that we can talk to God, that despite the infinite qualitative difference between creature and Creator, communication is nonetheless possible. There is no shame in asking God for things. Here are some of the things we ask God for, in the burial service, grounded in the access to truth that Christian faith gives:

- We ask God to accept our prayers on behalf of the departed person, by name. This implies that we believe the departed person is still a reality, that she still has her name, and that she continues to be an object of God's concern.

- Most specifically, in the opening collect we ask God to "grant *her* an entrance into the land of light and joy, in the fellowship of thy saints."[10]

- We ask God that every person baptized into Christ's death and resurrection "may die to sin and rise to newness of life" and that "through the grave and gate of death we may pass with him to our joyful resurrection." Note here the conditional "may": we do not claim more than we know; we do not claim, for instance, that every baptized person, or even just this person who has died, will pass with Christ to a joyful resurrection. Still we ask.[11]

- We ask God on behalf of us who have not yet died that we may grow in holiness and righteousness, be cleansed from all our sins, and serve God with "a quiet mind."[12]

- We ask God to console mourners with his love, which comes from his "fatherly care."[13]

---

10. Page 470. This is the collect for the burial office in the 1979 Book. New to the 1928 Book, there this was an optional additional prayer for the departed's soul.

11. Page 480; new to the 1979 Book.

12. Page 481. These petitions, now part of the standard intercessions, revise an additional optional prayer first in the 1892 Book.

13. Page 481.

- We ask God for ourselves and for everyone who has "died in the hope of the resurrection," that we may all "have our consummation and bliss in thy eternal and everlasting glory," and that we may join with all the saints and "receive the crown of life which thou dost promise to all who share in the victory of thy Son Jesus Christ."[14]

- Finally, at the graveside, or wherever else the body is "committed," this is said: "In sure and certain hope of the resurrection to eternal life through our Lord Jesus Christ, we commend to Almighty God our *sister N.*; and we commit *her* body to the ground (*or the deep, or the* *elements, or its resting place*); earth to earth, ashes to ashes, dust to dust. The Lord bless *her* and keep *her*, the Lord make his face to shine upon *her* and be gracious unto *her*, the Lord lift up his countenance upon *her* and give *her* peace."[15] The language of blessing is performative supplication: it is equivalent to "May the Lord bless her," which is in effect the point of the whole service. It is indeed the performative benediction that the Lord told Moses to have Aaron pronounce over the people—which is rightly translated in the singular—"The Lord bless *thee*" (Num 6:24); having had God's name "put" upon her, she becomes one of the many recipients of God's promise: "I will bless *them*" (Num 6:27).

- And then God is asked to give rest to the departed. "Multiply, we beseech thee, to those who rest in Jesus the manifold blessings of thy love, that the good work which thou didst begin in them may be made perfect unto the day of Jesus Christ."[16]

Now there are many additional, optional prayers, some of which are explicitly purgatorial. Yet even without considering them, there are already many

14. Page 481. The petition that we along with the faithful departed may receive, at the coming of God's kingdom, "our perfect consummation and bliss, both in body and soul, in thy eternal and everlasting glory" is in every Book used in the U.S. and its antecedent colonies since 1662, and is repeated with only slight modification in the additional prayers in the 1979 Book. In Rite II, "consummation" becomes "fulfilment" and "both in body and soul" drops out. But in Rite I the robust, full text remains; see p. 488.

15. Page 485. This language is in all Books from 1662, but is rearranged in 1979 to begin with "sure and certain hope." The Aaronic blessing, however, introduced in 1928 as the conclusion of the service, here in 1979 replaces a variously-worded affirmation that at Christ's coming our bodies will be made glorious like his.

16. Page 486; new to the 1928 Book.

significant conclusions we can draw about what the burial liturgy's prayers say and do not say.

First, at every turn the prayers call upon God's promises, and particularly the promises implicit in Jesus' victory of the cross. They never call upon the person's achievements. The need for Christian pilgrims to be cleansed from sin and to walk in holiness is affirmed, but it is not affirmed that this was achieved in any significant way by the departed. It is assumed, however, that "good work" did begin in the departed, a beginning which nonetheless is attributed to God's agency.

Second, the Christian hope is articulated as an entrance into a land of light and joy as a member of a company of saints. This is understood as true human flourishing (our "consummation"). It is a place where one receives a "crown of life" which, I take it, also symbolizes human flourishing: a land where one is really alive.

Still, none of this is assumed to have happened already. Indeed, that two-fold distinction is affirmed, the distinction that N. T. Wright has taught us, between "life after death" and "life after life after death."[17] The departed is now resting in Jesus, but there is yet to come "the day of Jesus Christ." This is spelled out in one of the prayers—optional in the 1979 Book, but mandated in the 1662, 1789, and 1892 Books and although optional in 1928 still printed in the main body of the service. I give it to you in its entirety in the current Rite I version (which is unchanged from 1789):

> Almighty God, with whom do live the spirits of those who depart hence in the Lord, and with whom the souls of the faithful, after they are delivered from the burden of the flesh, are in joy and felicity: We give thee hearty thanks for the good examples of all those thy servants, who, having finished their course in faith, do now rest from their labors. And we beseech thee that we, with all those who are departed in the true faith of thy holy Name, may have our perfect consummation and bliss, both in body and soul, in thy eternal and everlasting glory; through Jesus Christ our Lord.[18]

The prayer says, first, that those who "depart" from this world "in the Lord" have "joy and felicity" because they have been "delivered from the burden of the flesh." This is "flesh" in the Pauline sense of humanity in its

17. The latter, I have heard him say, was his preferred title for a recent book. His publishers, however, prevailed, and the book is known as *Surprised by Hope* (New York: HarperOne, 2008).

18. Page 488.

state of sinful opposition to the Lord; it is not our "body" properly understood but rather "the burden" that comes to us as children of sinful Adam. By contrast, towards the end the prayer makes a future request, that everyone who has true faith may have "perfect consummation and bliss, both in body and soul." There it is: the Christian expectation that there awaits for all the faithful a perfect fulfilment of their humanity as "body and soul" together, sinless and joyful in the glory of God.

How then would one preach this? I think, taking it all together, that it is possible to give a perfectly good funeral sermon in a minute or so. Here goes:

> We are here today because we knew, and loved, and now miss dear George. Many of you have precious memories of him, and some of you have told me that he touched you in important ways in your life. Yet more deeply, we are here today because of God. God gave George life, and now we stand at the verge of that unfathomable mystery: life has been taken away. Christian faith has a very strong hope, that when a person who believes in Jesus dies, Jesus takes that person to himself. The burden of this life is over, and today we ask God that George may rest in Jesus. This, however, is not the last word about George, or about any of us. We also hope for a future day, when everyone who believes will become a full human being, that our bodies will be raised from the dead. When that great day comes, we pray God that each of us, and George himself, may be there in what will be our perfect consummation and bliss.

One would, of course, flesh this out somewhat. But my aim is to give an example of speaking mercifully and truthfully at once: not to suggest either that George is going to heaven (or indeed already there) or that it is a certainty that he will rise to glory; and yet neither do I wish to suggest any limits to God's salvific will.

But what about preaching hell?

As you have learned, I would not do so either during the Triduum or at a funeral. But I do think the preacher should have some clear theological principles about hell, and that these should be preached from time to time as befits the lectionary.

The first theological principle is this. While it may be possible that all persons will be saved, and that universal salvation may be compatible with Christian doctrine, there are no guarantees on this. Which is to say, it is possible for a human being not to be saved. Indeed, it is possible that I might not be saved. And, not to put too fine a point on it, it is possible that you might not be saved.

The Bible does not sidestep the possibility that a human being can make a decisive wrong-turn leading to punishment and death. A harrowing chapter in this regard (although it does not speak of eternal punishment) is Deut 13, which I don't believe occurs in contemporary Sunday lectionaries, but does appear in the daily office. In this part of Moses' preparatory admonitions to the people before they enter the promised land, he says that if ever in the future anyone urge them to turn away from the Lord and go to other gods, that person is to be put to death. It will not matter if the person is a prophet who performs signs of his power or authorization; there can never be any sign that would signify it is right to turn away from the Lord. And it does not matter if that person is your parent or your sibling or even your child, he or she is to be put to death, and you are to cast the first stone. Indeed, this is one of the few places where the Scriptures use the word "friend": if your friend "who is as your own soul" urges you to turn away from the Lord, you must not do so, and your friend must be executed.

The reason for this severe teaching, I believe, is that idolatry in the end is not just a mistake, like looking off in the distance and thinking you see a man but when you walk closer it turns out to be a tree, or like the mistake of thinking McDonald's hamburgers are better than Wendy's. In the end, idolatry means the oppression and death of human beings. Ezekiel makes it clear: to worship the idols is to acquiesce in the sacrifice of children. Robert Jenson writes, "Just one excavated area at the Phoenician colony at Carthage contains the ashes of 40,000 sacrificed infants. I have been there and never forgotten it."[19] The deep reason why idolatry means human sacrifice, Herbert McCabe says, is that all the other gods are beings within the universe, and to worship them is to lose freedom and to submit to violence and oppression. They are not really gods, these baals, but instead they are powerful bullies and they drink blood.[20]

19. Commenting on Ezek 20:31. Robert W. Jenson, *Ezekiel*, Brazos Theological Commentary on the Bible (Grand Rapids: Brazos, 2009) 158n3.

20. See his essay "The God of Truth," in *God Still Matters*, edited by Brian Davies (London: Continuum, 2002) 29–35.

To be saved is to be delivered from the false gods and to worship the Lord, who is the Creator of the universe, who causes us to act freely,[21] who offers us our consummation and bliss as human beings, body and soul together, in the kingdom of God. One may truly characterize such a life as one of perfect *caritas* (love). And *caritas* is in the end friendship with God and with all of God's friends.[22] So we may speak of our fulfillment as being found as human beings living as friends together.

Is it indeed possible to turn one's back on all that? Is it possible to make a departure from the Lord that is at the same time a decisive turning away from human friendship? I believe it is. And the preacher's task is to try to imagine what it is like to do so. What might I say in a sermon, then? That if a person says, "I don't want to be friends with other people; I want to be alone," and if that person takes small steps to cut herself off from others, and then larger steps, and finally decisively chooses for herself over all other people and everything, she is going to hell. The essence of sin is separation, the desire to achieve solitary self-sufficiency. Sin is the desire to live apart from God (making my own decisions about what's good and evil, which is in the end to deny that I am a creature of God [cf. Gen 3:5]). And correlatively, which is in the end the same thing, sin is the desire to live apart from others. You know how C. S. Lewis depicted hell? It was a grey town where people kept moving farther and farther apart.

Are there people who really desire such isolation, who "love" themselves so much that they hate everything else? We do not know if any person will persist to the end in such a state. But to examine honestly the cruelty of our world is to face squarely that it may be. In the United States, something like one out of every one or two hundred adults is incarcerated, and one out of three or four children conceived is aborted. Are these just mistakes about who is a human being and how human beings should be treated? Or do they signify that dreadful choice away from friendship and towards damnation? In fact, it is probably in some cases the one, and in some cases the other. Turn to the Middle East. We may be about to see Sunnis and Shiites kill off a few million of each other. What if the thought creeps into our mind, that such a war, while regrettable, may well leave things better

21. As Aquinas teaches us. It is not to the point of this paper, but another important topic for homiletic and pedagogical efforts is to teach the truth that our freedom is enhanced by God's causality. The illusion that I achieve freedom by distancing myself from God, or that God makes me free by distancing himself from me, is a pernicious illusion.

22. As Aquinas also teaches; Aquinas famously defined *caritas* as friendship with God.

for us? Or to take it another way, can we imagine lobbing a bomb through a window (of a capitalist, or an abortionist, or an arms manufacturer—it makes no difference) and justifying that action to ourselves?

The homiletic objective will be to raise questions, to lure people into the realization that they, too, could make (and may be making) choices against God and neighbor, choices that could result in eternal loss. The sermon does not aim to persuade conclusively about any given issue (we must always leave open the possibility of our own ignorance, just as others may act from ignorance, and we also must hope ever for repentance and conversion of life). But it is true that any one of us might fail of our humanity, reject grace decisively, and end in perdition. That, the preacher must not avoid saying.

Finally, a word about heaven. The old tag has it that one would choose heaven for the climate but hell for the company. That is a canard: hell is boring and uninteresting in the extreme. But, still, people need help imagining how heaven can be interesting. If we're just strumming harps and sitting on clouds, wouldn't that be rather boring?

So try to consider what it means for human beings to flourish. Picture for yourself and for your people what it could mean for human beings to act together without the frictions and subtractions caused by sin. Instead of having to worry about thieves and, when burglarized, spend much labor on restoring the mess as best one can, one would have that time and energy for productive activity. That's just one example. Everything we do together we could do better and to a higher degree if we weren't encumbered by sin. Orchestras would play better. Inventors would make more new things. Human creativity, in the service of human good, would multiply without end.

"Come farther up, come farther in!" That's the ecstatic summons to the blessed in C. S. Lewis's *Last Battle*, and it points to the reality that our consummation and bliss is not in stasis but in human activity, great human activity, cooperative enterprises in which each human being flourishes uniquely and yet socially. That is the new earth, the earth that has been married to heaven, the unending joy of people, body and soul together, who are supremely actualized as God-made and God-redeemed human beings.

www.ingramcontent.com/pod-product-compliance
Lightning Source LLC
Chambersburg PA
CBHW020211090426
42734CB00008B/1025